TOMORROW

The profound crisis affecting our societies is obvious. Ecological disturbances, social exclusion, the rampant exploitation of natural resources, the frenetic and dehumanizing quest for profit, and the widening of inequalities lie at the heart of our contemporary problems.

Nevertheless, men and women everywhere are coming together around innovative and original projects with a view to opening up new prospects for the future. There are solutions. Novel proposals are being made all over the planet, often on a small scale, but always with the aim of bringing about real change in our societies.

THE TRANSITION STARTS HERE, NOW AND TOGETHER

From the same authors

Lionel Astruc
Vandana Shiva: Creative Civil Disobedience. Tomorrow, Actes Sud, 2017

Rob Hopkins
The Transition Handbook: From Oil Dependency to Local Resilience,
Green Books, 2008
*The Transition Companion: Making Your Community More Resilient in
Uncertain Times,* Green Books, 2011
The Power of Just Doing Stuff: How Local Action Can Change the World,
Green Books, 2013
*21 Stories of Transition: How a Movement of Communities Is Coming
Together to Reimagine and Rebuild Our World,* Transition Network, 2015
*The Essential Guide to Doing Transition: Getting Transition Started in
Your Street, Community, Town or Organization,* Transition Network,
2017 (www.transitionnetwork.org)

Edited by Cyril Dion

Originally published in French as
Le pouvoir d'agir ensemble, ici et maintenant, by Actes Sud in 2015.

ROB HOPKINS
LIONEL ASTRUC

THE TRANSITION STARTS HERE, NOW AND TOGETHER

INTERVIEWS

TRANSLATED BY LISA DAVIDSON

TOMORROW
ACTES SUD

ACKNOWLEDGMENTS

The unbridled enthusiasm of the Transition movement stands in stark contrast to the emptiness of our ambient consumerism. Its founders share an imperceptible, yet crucial characteristic: they are lighthearted, unaffected by the apathy toward the urgency of our environmental situation. Rob Hopkins embodies this infectious energy, and I would like to extend special thanks to him for what he transmitted to me in Totnes: a deep-seated optimism, a message that transcends words.

I would not have been able to express all this in this book without the help of Marie-Marie Andrasch and Cyril Dion–another tireless guiding spirit to whom I owe so much–whose corrections and suggestions considerably improved the initial version of the text.

I am fortunate to live in the Trièves (at the borders of the Écrins and the Vercors), home to many firm believers in Transition and others who aren't, who nevertheless devote countless hours to their community, and to its resilience, culture, and life. Thanks to them: once you've crossed the Col de Cornillon, everything is different, and I send them all my warmest greetings.

LIONEL ASTRUC

To Romy, Gaspard, and Nina.

To Philippe Poncet, a genius mechanic
and philosopher, explorer,
and photographer of silence

INTRODUCTION

Outside our comfort zones

Among the billions of videos uploaded to YouTube, one of them—a poor-quality, cell-phone recording—shows small groups of people at a rock festival, scattered around a large field in the early afternoon, enjoying the music. A man gets up and starts dancing, utterly unconcerned that everyone is looking at him. His infectious happiness and goofy dancing are compelling. A second dancer joins in. Others follow, and finally, everyone gets in the act. But this is only the beginning, and for three long minutes, dozens, then hundreds of festival-goers rush toward the growing crowd. A nonstop flow of people streams past the camera as an undulating crowd fills up what started out as a large, grassy hill.[1]

Rob Hopkins loves this video. It demonstrates the powerful ripple effect generated by the simple act of taking a step, of one individual setting something in motion. He says: "The bravest one is not the dancer at the start. It was the first few people who joined in. They legitimized him, which was an essential, inestimable step, setting an example for the others." He may be downplaying the protagonist, but let's face facts: despite his well-mannered demeanor, Rob Hopkins could very well be that improbable dancer who decides to stand up and sweep others along in his wake—specifically concerning local initiatives to combat climate change and to build a new, more supportive society; and to support efforts by communities to retake control of key local issues, such as food, energy, finance, housing, and so on.

One day in 2005, he too decided to leave his comfort zone, to try to engage the people around him in exploring a different model of change, one that proposed that they get together to organize nothing less than a new, locally based economy: a new model that could effectively withstand both environmental and economic crises, while

1. This video was shown at a TED conference in 2010: Derek Sivers, "How to Start a Movement," TED, February 2010, 3:10: http://www.ted.com/talks/derek_sivers_how_to_start_a_movement.

planning for a post-oil, post-growth world. An economy that would harness the resources at hand: people would no longer expect food to arrive from the other side of the planet at great fuel costs, but instead create short food supply chains and cultivate all the available land (gardens, rooftops, municipal parks); they would no longer complain about pollution, but unite their neighbors around a project of local renewable energy cooperatives; no longer rail against the banks and the stock markets, but adopt a local currency that promotes solidarity and enriches the community; and no longer let the usual promoters construct energy-guzzling, exorbitantly priced houses, but form a collective of "citizen promoters" to build affordable housing using local materials. And it had to be fun.

To implement this transformation of society, Rob Hopkins doesn't depend on support from any corporation or politician. "Let's not wait for the cavalry to arrive," he says, "because they're not coming. What if we, ourselves, are the cavalry?" Local people are the key to Transition: this movement, midway between everyday environmental actions and large-scale political decisions, mobilizes people who want to act on a street, neighborhood, or city level. The success of this initiative, developed in Totnes, United Kingdom, was so great that it spread to forty-seven countries in just a few years. This raises the question of the idea that led Rob Hopkins to dream up Transition Initiatives. Where did it come from?

"I want to be able to tell them that I did everything I could"

In 2005, Rob Hopkins was an ordinary, low-profile guy in his thirties, unknown to the public at large. His view was that oil and globalization were the root of many of the crises endangering humanity. All over the world, the history of the last few decades has been tangled up in this issue. Oil, which has been used since the Industrial Revolution to increase production, facilitate the movement of goods, and feed a growing population, quickly plunged society into a runaway consumerism. The damage inflicted by this transformation has been so great that we are now in a new epoch, dubbed Anthropocene, characterized by humanity's impact on the biosphere. It has affected the geology of the earth itself, the lithosphere. Like the earth, our air has also been badly polluted: the ongoing and massive emission of greenhouse gases is accelerating global warming, an assessment that has garnered near unanimous support. Despite widespread awareness, everyone also knows that, despite the regular publication of alarming and ever-more specific reports, the solutions implemented by politicians over the last thirty years have fallen far short of meeting the scope of the challenge.

To this environmental overview, Rob Hopkins added the economic havoc caused by cheap oil: this raw material has allowed multinationals to flood local communities with low-cost products from distant countries via supermarket chain stores, substituting the traditional short food supply chains for long ones; local prosperity for unemployment; resilience for fragility. He compares large-scale retailers to extractive industries, like mining companies, which scoop up local wealth. To illustrate this phenomenon, Fiona Ward of Transition Town Totnes wrote the Totnes Local Economic Blueprint, one of the seminal documents of Transition. According to this study, prior to the launch of the Transition movement, of the 30 million pounds spent on food every year in the town of Totnes, 22 million ended up in the cash registers of the supermarkets. Yet if people shifted just 10% of the money they spent in large chain stores to local businesses, they would inject 2 million pounds every year into the local economy. This money–a considerable sum for a town of 8,500 people–could not only return prosperity to the community, it could also empower the population considerably: "When all the food you eat comes from a chain store, you imperceptibly incorporate the fact that you have no influence on the economy," says Rob Hopkins. With short supply chains, on the other hand, residents once again have a voice in the process, regardless of the economic sector. This blueprint also pinpointed the immense fragility of communities that depend on distant supply structures over which they have no control: a single transport strike, an economic crisis, or even a disruption to the supply of energy resources are all it takes to create shortages within just a few days.

These findings–describing an all-mighty system based on long supply chains, along with injunctions from climate scientists not to exceed an increase in global warming of more than 2° Celsius[1]– triggered a sense of urgency in Rob Hopkins's life: "I have four children, and later I want to be able to tell them that during this critical period, when we still had a window in which to act, I did absolutely everything in my power and devoted every hour of my day to finding a solution." This awareness gave him, a man with no notoriety and no resources, the possibility of achieving an extraordinary feat: to quietly transform his town through grassroots action; to make it more autonomous and more resilient to the crises looming in the future; and to construct a global network of "ordinary people" working to create an alternative, a fabric of communities that could offer solutions to the crises in the event the system does indeed collapse. To spread the ideas of Transition around the world, Rob Hopkins decided to teach by example, putting his trust in the power of a good idea and a true story, that of Totnes.

People reinventing their lives

Before setting out to meet the people in his community, and then creating the Transition Town movement, Rob Hopkins had been

1. This figure comes from successive assessments published by the Intergovernmental Panel on Climate Change (IPCC); the fifth report, "Climate Change 2014: Impacts, Adaptation, and Vulnerability," is available at http://www.ipcc.ch/report/ar5/wg2/.

the first person to teach permaculture–at Kinsale College in Ireland–as part of a full-fledged program. This method, which deals nominally with agriculture, has a much larger scope: it aims to not only harness local resources, but more broadly speaking, to create farms and communities as autonomous ecosystems that are both energy and labor efficient and productive. The goal is to create resilience: the ability to persist (the word "permaculture" comes from "permanent culture"), despite external events and changes. Each plant, each configuration, and each piece of equipment, is designed and positioned to interact in the best possible way with the others, just as everything is interconnected in nature. Waste from one becomes a resource for another, so that the whole is far greater than its parts.[1]

The globalization that governs trade is the exact opposite of permaculture: our local economies now depend on resources that come from far away, reaching communities via major retailers whose profits are channeled to shareholders uninterested in local issues rather than used to finance local projects. In recent decades, the social fabric and local economies, as well as relationships between producers and consumers, and among individuals, have crumbled. As a result, Rob Hopkins decided to use permaculture methods, applying them not only to farms, but to villages, small towns, and districts, so that each area can reclaim its wealth, its creativity, and its productivity. This idea was first promoted by the founders of permaculture, David Holmgren and Bill Mollison,[2] but had never been put into practice on such a large scale as that of the Transition movement.

1. These principles are explained in the following books: Bill Mollison and David Holmgren, *Permaculture One: A Perennial Agricultural System for Human Settlements* (Sister's Creek Tagari, 1990) and *Permaculture 2* (Sister's Creek: Tagari, 2011); and Perrine and Charles Hervé-Gruyer, *Miraculous Abundance* (White River Junction: Chelsea Green, 2016).
2. Bill Mollison and David Holmgren, *Permaculture One: A Perennial Agricultural System for Human Settlements* (Sister's Creek: Tagari, 1990).

After he worked long and hard explaining this new vision, the Transition project generated a great deal of enthusiasm among many residents of Totnes. The action groups created to look at such issues as food, energy, and the economy, led to a myriad of initiatives. Shared gardens flourished throughout this pretty little town, which even allotted areas in the public parks to vegetable gardens and fruit production. One-third of the households participating in the movement's "Transition Street" initiative have installed solar panels on their roofs; 195 companies accept and use the local currency, the Totnes Pound (including 160 that use the paper version and 35 the electronic version); local grains are once again processed and milled in a crowdfunded processing unit; and a regular forum brings together people proposing environmental and resilient local projects with possible investors from the community. In short, an economic and social biodiversity has been revived in the years since the start of Transition Town Totnes.

Around the world by word-of-mouth

A global network was created from this first Transition experience, with only rudimentary communication tools and the smallest possible staff (just eleven employees). This massive and spontaneous expansion is rooted in the success of the Totnes initiative. The territories (towns, villages, neighborhoods) inspired by this idea now form a network consisting of 1,500 Transition groups (including 400 in the UK), involving tens of thousands of "Transitioners." Many of them have pursued this approach even further than Totnes: in Bristol, for example, 800 companies accept the complementary currency launched in the city–including the former mayor, who received his salary in Bristol Pounds; in Liège (in the Wallonia region of Belgium), a co-op of 1,200 residents planted 30 acres of grapes and is about to produce more than 100,000 bottles of wine. And in Bath (Somerset, UK), a group of people created a large, socially responsible energy production company: after several share issues (including one for 2 million pounds), the residents became owners of their energy production. Bath and West Community Energy produces electricity locally from solar panels installed on the rooftops of public buildings and schools. Smaller initiatives by Transition groups are also powerful stimuli, whether they involve an orchard of 190 trees in Saint-Quentin-en-Yvelines (France), solar panels (10kW) on a church in Melbourne (Australia), or the shared gardens and bakery in Brasilândia, a favela in São Paulo (Brazil).[1]

These hundreds of projects happened by word-of-mouth, via the Internet. Yet the movement does not have any well-planned marketing strategy; some people may be perplexed that the Transition movement's communication materials and designs are relatively minimal. The power of Transition's expansion comes from this alternative story: a story that beckons to the best of who we are, that touches a bubble of hope buried under years of resignation and the disappointments of "economic realism." Merely talking about the Totnes experience generates enthusiasm; people immediately feel like joining in and talking about it to others. In the last few years, this adventure seems to have been relayed along a frequency that has nothing to do with major TV channels, but one that connects people directly to the movement. It's not so much a matter of calculation as it is Rob Hopkins's belief in the power of a positive story to motivate people to act. "Our civilization is very good at imagining its own destruction, notably through countless stories and films about the end of the world. But where are the stories that talk about our incredible creativity and our mobilization to solve problems? Can we manage to represent a low-carbon world? That's what Transition is about!"

1. These examples are also in Rob Hopkins's book, *The Power of Just Doing Stuff: How Local Action Can Change the World* (Cambridge: UIT Cambridge, Ltd., 2013).

This new story, about combating global warming, is an opportunity to leave behind the idea of "always more" and head instead for "always better." It's an unusual approach to an issue that is too often overshadowed by a prevailing sense of gloom. Transition does not promise miracles, nor a spectacular turnaround. It starts with our everyday lives and our limitations, but above all, the unimagined capacities we all have within us. It speaks directly to all of us in simple and utterly realistic terms. It brings together neighbors who once passed each other by without speaking, people who now sit together around a table or on the steps of their building, to organize a carpooling plan with other residents on their street or to replace the ubiquitous flowerbeds with a shared vegetable plot. One thing leads to another, and gradually these initiatives spread to other neighborhoods and get the attention of town councils.

What impact on our current model?

This story is only powerful because it can be "seen, felt, and touched," as Rob Hopkins says. The leaders of the movement are not wide-eyed storytellers: their priorities–local initiatives–are grounded in reality. But can this approach truly defuse the never-ending cycle of crises we are experiencing? Can Transition groups profoundly change the system? How do they prevent multinationals from continuing to seize natural resources? Is this not just a parallel, inconsequential path alongside the trajectory of the giant agribusiness, energy, and finance sectors? Furthermore, does Transition factor in the concerns of people living in need?

Rob Hopkins tries to answer these questions in the following interview. He discusses how poor neighborhoods in London and São Paulo have successfully adopted the Transition movement–so much so that the poorest people are willing to invest their time and money to garden or install solar panels on their roofs. He also talks about national law. In terms of the alleged power of multi-nationals, what would happen if we no longer supported them? If instead, most of our purchases benefited prosperous, job-creating local businesses? This overview shows the real benefits of Transition, by demonstrating the real and tangible power of ordinary people.

The path to Transition

This book covers the background of the Transition movement, in the words of the man who launched it. The first section explores the unique context in which this idea first germinated. Rob Hopkins discusses the long path that led to Totnes, via three years in a Buddhist monastery in Tuscany, a journey through Asia, and a job teaching permaculture in an Irish college. He then describes the work accomplished with his friends in Totnes–including the nitty-gritty aspects–the enthusiasm of residents for Transition, and the successive initiatives undertaken to transform the town. The second section examines the mystery of the spontaneous spread of the movement. We look at the factors that contributed to this planetary success, achieved with minimal resources: a lean structure without power struggles, the ability to make delocalization a global message and to mobilize beyond an activist core group, as well as the capacity to motivate younger people. All this helped with the extraordinary spread of the movement. But what are the implications of all this? How will Transition impact the systems in which it evolves? The final section deals with these issues and demonstrates, using real-life examples, how this movement bolsters democracy, frees up people, influences laws, and alters our ideas of innovation. At an even deeper level, Transition encourages all of us, as individuals, to reconnect to the earth and to ourselves, even if only by relearn-ing basic skills.

Although he holds a doctorate[1] and has been inspired by authors ranging from Fritjof Capra to Charles Dickens, Rob Hopkins comes across as a singularly humble guy, evident in his self-deprecating sense of humor and his myriad references. His answers range from stories about the new bank note featuring an image of David Bowie (an actual fact, on the Brixton pound) to Queen Elizabeth throwing stones at the windows of the founders of local currencies (which do not feature her crowned head), an importer of Chinese-made plastic toilet seats who should re-examine his life, and an intriguing theory called the "doughnut effect" which, to explain the mobiliza-tion of the Transition movement, refers to "keeping jam inside the doughnut." This vision, so different from the ever-so-professional seriousness and solemnity of other NGOs, may throw some people off. But it is deliberate, and indeed, is even one of the cornerstones of this movement, which aims to replace too much grandstanding, too much information, with practical initiatives. Transition wants to remain fun, spontaneous, and dynamic, much to the delight of participants who enjoy spending time together. This straightforward approach reconnects us to our everyday issues, and invites everyone to tackle social and environmental problems: Transition is a real world, where people are happy to finally face reality, where every-one finally gets up and joins the dance.

LIONEL ASTRUC

---

1. "Localisation and Resilience at the Local Level: The Case of Transition Town Totnes (Devon, UK)," University of Plymouth, 2010: http://transitionculture.org/shop/localisation-and-resilience-at-the-local-level-the-case-of-transition-town-totnes/.

1

TOTNES: THE ENVIRONMENTAL SAGA OF A SMALL TOWN

An English high-school student, an Italian farmer, and a Buddhist monastery

Lionel Astruc: Can you tell us about the journey that transformed you, a young British citizen, into a permaculture teacher in the Irish countryside?

Rob Hopkins: This journey, which lasted several years, started when I was eighteen. I had just finished high school, living in Bristol in a flat with three friends. We were broke, and our future in a Great Britain undermined by unemployment wasn't looking good. We started working, doing odd jobs to make enough money to leave the country, and then all went traveling off in different directions, setting each other the challenge of finding a way to stay out of England. At the time, we could travel all over Europe with cheap rail passes. Two of us ended up back at home, with no money, and the third guy went to a Buddhist monastery in Tuscany. He kept sending us these postcards saying how amazing it was, telling us to come as soon as possible. So the next summer I did, not because I was interested in Buddhism, but because I wanted to learn how to meditate. I was bored with city life, including all the partying. I wanted to learn how my mind worked, how to be more in control of it—and I ended staying at the monastery for three years.

LA: What was your day-to-day life like, and how did it challenge your ideas about ecology?

RH: Room and board, and meditation classes were free in exchange for work. When I arrived, the house manager, a guy named Alessandro, showed me everything I had to do: sweep the stairs and wash the floors, that kind of thing. Everything was going well, until three weeks later, when Alessandro had to go to Elba Island.

"Are you leaving?" I asked him. "Who's going to take care of the house?" "You are," he said. "Here are the keys."

I was eighteen and had never really held any position of responsibility before. I was quite disorganized as a teenager, and suddenly I had to manage the logistics for a 140-bed hotel, with groups of several dozen people constantly coming and going. It was best thing that ever happened to me. This experience was just extraordinary.

I learned a lot about certain things that were dysfunctional with life at the monastery: I grew frustrated with a community that talked about "working for the happiness of all living beings," but then threw out all this garbage; that the community only grew a tiny portion of the food they ate. I think much has changed since then, but at the time I was struck by this disconnect. During this period, I became intrigued by the idea of bringing that compassionate approach to the sustainable management of resources. I understood that altruism inevitably translates into protecting the environment, because we all depend on the natural resources and good health of the planet.

During my time at the monastery, a farmer from a nearby village—Pomaia, about half an hour from Pisa, up in the hills—used to stop by and ask us to help out. He didn't know it, but with him, we were able to participate in some of the last years of a true peasant agriculture. This guy, Guido, was about eighty years old, and he was as wide as he was tall, with calloused hands like spades, baked dark by the sun. He ran his farm alone, and on top of the produce he sold, he grew most of his own food, including the grapes for his wine. He had a horse (called Dora), a cow, and some chickens. He kind of adopted me and taught me Italian. He drove an ancient tractor; we hung on to the back of it, sowing seeds and planting, while he drove and shouted out incomprehensible instructions. He'd done this all his life, while we were just useless city kids from England. He worked all day and all night to keep his farm going. He left a lasting impression on me, I was very impressed by the integrity of his life and his work. This experience in Italy was very formative, and the seeds of Transition came, in part, from this trip I took in the 1990s.

LA: In short, you chose an education provided by monks and farmers rather than university professors. That's an interesting choice for a young eighteen-year-old.

RH: Yes, for me, this experience was like attending university. At that age, leaving my home and country behind, being giving responsibilities, learning the discipline of a meditation practice among people of such integrity, was an extraordinarily formative experience.

At that time, an entire generation of Tibetan lamas had fled Tibet, which had been invaded by China, and crossed the Himalayas on foot. They had grown up in the monasteries and memorized all the ancient texts. The Chinese destroyed six thousand monasteries and burned mounds of books. Once the refugees reached India, they transcribed all these texts from memory, thereby saving entire libraries. I thought this was phenomenal! I met many of them when I was living in Tuscany, especially during festivals. I had come just to learn about meditation, but once I met these monks, I became more deeply interested in Buddhism. I was especially drawn to the idea of the bodhisattva,[1] whose life is devoted to serving others. Buddhists also explain that if something is not right, the solution is to first search within oneself before blaming someone else. Later on, this powerful idea became the cornerstone of my approach to ecology, and is an essential component of the Transition movement. In an era when many people simply criticize politicians and multinationals without acting within their own sphere, Transition offers people a way to look at what they can do,

---

1. In Sanskrit, *bodhi* means "enlightened," while *sattva* means "being." For Buddhists a bodhisattva is a person who devotes his or her life to achieving enlightenment through service.

collectively, to reinvent an everyday existence that is more compatible with our climate issues and that creates stronger social bonds.

LA: Why did you leave the monastery?

RH: The people there offered me a small job in India: they were organizing a Buddhist festival and asked me to be responsible for selling tea during the event. I ended up traveling for a year and a half in India, China, and Tibet. I met my wife there, and we went to England, where I learned permaculture, first near Bristol, then to Ireland, where I taught for ten years, from 1996 to 2005. Initially, I was teaching informal evening classes and helping to create the first ecovillage in the country. Then I thought it would be great to create a permaculture course at the college, an official one-year program that anyone could take, exactly like registering for a traditional math, sociology, or history class. There weren't any university programs like this at the time, so I had to create the syllabus for the class from scratch. A friend of mine who was teaching drama at Kinsale College suggested that I propose my project to this very progressive institution. The principal said he'd never heard of permaculture before, but he was curious. "Do you think you can get fifteen people who'd be interested in this subject?" he asked, a bit skeptically. I assured him I could, so he gave the go-ahead.

The first year we had twenty-four people, and every year after that we had thirty-five to forty people. In fact, the course was full even before class registration started. After three years, we added an optional second year to the initial one-year program, because people wanted to stay on and learn more. It was very hands-on, very practical: ponds to harvest rainwater, small straw-bale houses, vegetable gardens. When we started the course, the college was surrounded by grass and lawns. It was entirely transformed; we planted orchards, built a polytunnel, and even a natural amphitheater made from all local materials—a project we did the last year

I was there. The role played by the college principal and his way of running things were crucial: he really trusted us, and if the last thing you had done worked, he'd readily give his approval for the next one. So the last year, when we asked if we could pull down the bicycle shed and build a natural amphitheater, he said OK after I showed him a little sketch I had made on the back of an envelope, at the last minute. Anywhere else, I would have had to do a risk assessment, get plans from an architect, draw up a budget, and so on. But he never asked for any of that. This college was therefore a very fertile place, where, without yet knowing it, I was planting the seeds for a much larger project.

Applying permaculture principles to the economy

LA: In 2004, you asked your students to use the principles of permaculture to respond to the challenge of peak oil. How did this work?

RH: At the end of the year at Kinsale College, a friend gave me a video called *The End of Suburbia*,[1] a documentary about peak oil that describes the collapse of the American dream after all the fossil fuel reserves have been depleted. Dr. Colin Campbell, former oil company geologist and founder of the Association for the Study of Peak Oil. I rang him up and asked him to talk to my students, who watched the film and listened to Campbell's talk on the first day of class the following year.

This film and his participation made it all very real for me. Before, my mental picture about oil was that it would flow steadily until it just suddenly stopped, and then the last drop would fall and that

1. *End of Suburbia*: http://www.endofsuburbia.com/

would be it, the last drop would drip out of a gas station somewhere in the heartland of America. The truth is that once the curve of oil production peaks, it then gradually drops off. Fascinated by this idea, I asked my students to apply the principles of permaculture to help create a scenario so that the town of Kinsale could achieve two related goals: first, move away from oil dependency to reach a place where it wasn't needed anymore; and second, to demonstrate to the local people that they would become better, healthier, and happier as a result. Around that time, I read David Holmgren's book *Permaculture: Principles and Pathways Beyond Sustainability*.[1] The author repositions this practice in the context of climate change and peak oil. He convincingly proposes that permaculture can provide a response: applying its major principles, notably to the economy and the organization of an entire society, can trigger the major transformation that we need.

I designed a program with my students based on these principles, to experiment with it around Kinsale. They went out and met lots of people who were already involved in the community, and then organized a first Open Space event. They worked in pairs: one set of people would do energy, another would take food, and so on. Their assignment was to produce an energy timetable pathway for Kinsale, based on permaculture principles. When they handed in their work, I was really impressed, and even more, excited, as it could definitively be put into practice.

LA: What did the reports contain?

RH: They were put together and formatted into a document called the *Kinsale Energy Descent Action Plan*.[2] It's a very specific scenario

1. David Holmgren, *Permaculture: Principles and Pathways Beyond Sustainability* (Heburn Springs: Holmgren Design Service, 2002).
2. "Kinsale 2021: An Energy Descent Action Plan–Version 1, 2005," http://transitionus.org/sites/default/files/KinsaleEnergyDescentActionPlan.pdf.

whereby this town of 7,000 people could make the transition from a high-energy consumption town to a low-energy one. The report looks at all the town's economic sectors: food, energy tourism, education, and health. In terms of food, for example, we realized that 90% of the food consumed in Kinsale–considered one of Ireland's culinary capitals–came from outside the area, from other regions. The students realized just how much a dependency on the transport of goods was worrisome and how vulnerable it made the area. The same holds true for many areas whose food supply comes from outside the region or from abroad. Given a strike by truck drivers, for example, areas like the city of London would start to face shortages in just a few days. We've already seen this, as with the blockade of English refineries in 2000. The owner of Sainsbury's supermarkets notified Prime Minister Tony Blair that if the blockade continued, food shortages would occur within days.[1] This dependency concerns all of us, including France, where regions like the Île-de-France only have enough reserves for several days in case of a blockade or a fuel shortage.[2] When my students started to look into this issue, the data I just mentioned didn't exist, but they understood the extreme fragility of our food supply system, this unbelievable lack of resilience.

LA: What proposals did they come up with?

RH: Once the current situation had been examined, the plan set forth goals for each sector. Concerning food: the vision aimed for more autonomy, by converting landscaped lawns maintained by the town into orchards and vegetable gardens, with fruit trees lining the streets, people trading seeds and cooking more fresh produce, which they purchased as much as possible from local producers.

---

1. "Fuel Crises Hit Services," BBC News, September 14, 2000.
2. Emmanuel Bailly, *Le Concept de l'écorégion* (Millançay: Intelligence verte, 2005).

The students then laid out practical steps, detailed year by year, to reach these goals. In the first year, the project supporters would organize an Open Space meeting for representatives of the food sector, along with all interested parties. These people would form a partnership to encourage relocalization. This group would then promote initiatives in the food sector. The second year, the members would produce a Local Food Action Plan for Kinsale, as well as a Directory of Local Food. At the same time, a Local Food Officer would work with this network, especially schools, so that by the second year, they would purchase 60% of their food from local producers, 40% of which would be organic. Finally, the participants would arrange a trip to visit Slow Food towns that are pursuing similar goals, in other places, to get a feel for their experience. During the third year, a local farmers market would be created; the town's maintenance staff would trained in permaculture techniques, and they would plant edible species like chestnuts and walnuts wherever possible. The local hospital would agree to using as many local products as possible in meals served to patients, and the students at Kinsale College would run awareness-raising projects in schools and create vegetable gardens.

LA: What did the students hope to achieve?

RH: The project should result in food autonomy by the year 2021; the path to reaching this goal involves a tremendous amount of creativity, along with a hefty dose of pragmatism. Specifically, they planned for the formation of an organic food co-op that includes local farmers, the creation of niche markets like medicinal mushrooms, and so on. The students also projected that relocalized food production would be a draw for tourism, with visitors identifying committed businesses though this label. As it turned out, this creative, ambitious approach flourished in each of the sectors covered in the report—housing, energy, etc.—by providing goals, followed by practical recommendations to reach them. In fact, this plan, drawn up by students as a simple homework assignment, is still a blueprint for the residents of Kinsale, and some of its goals have been achieved.[1] This report turned out to be visionary: it basically laid out the plans for all future Transition Initiatives.

LA: How did this project, conducted in a small Irish college, spread so rapidly and to so many countries around the world?

RH: I merely formatted the students' texts; we called it the *Kinsale Energy Descent Action Plan*, and in July 2005, just before I moved here, to Totnes, we organized a conference called "Fueling the Future." It was one of the first peak oil conferences held in Ireland, a seemingly minor event, but it ended up playing a decisive role. It was a real celebration of what we had done during the permaculture course. Richard Heinberg came; he is one of the world's most eminent specialists on peak oil and a senior fellow at the Post Carbon Institute, a think tank that advises organizations preparing for a post-oil era. Colin Campbell also attended the event.

We hadn't planned to publish it, but I had a bit of money left in my budget, so we printed five hundred copies of this brochure, without having the slightest idea that it could have any kind of impact. During the conference the reports were piled up in a corner of the room. We hadn't launched it or promoted it. But Richard Heinberg started speaking and was waving the document around: "This is extraordinary, this is remarkable, this is what all the people interested in peak oil need to read!" He went back home with a copy and told everybody about it; our printed copies sold out in two weeks. Someone even ordered one hundred copies from Australia. We put a version online, on the conference website. And from there it exploded, with thousands of downloads. Many people liked

1. *Transition Town Kinsale*, http://www.transitiontownkinsale.org.

the idea that we not only anticipated the end of oil, but that we proposed Transition as a positive solution to this impasse. At that time, if you googled "responses to peak oil," all you got was survivalist stuff, men heading up into the mountains with four years' worth of baked beans, tools, and guns. It was all very depressing. The lack of any other positive scenarios probably explains the success of this document.

This was my entire focus when I came to England and moved to Totnes in September 2005, even though I hadn't yet figured out how to implement it. But I realized, when rereading the report that we held a crucial piece of the puzzle. But how to pursue it? It was important to create a space where this concept could take shape and where we could implement this idea that inspired so many people.

Totnes as a laboratory of Transition: taking action

LA: How did you transform this information into action?

RH: During the period when lots of people were downloading the report, I decided to launch the "Transition Culture" blog. A lot of the early posts were discussions about this work: many readers said that it was extremely relevant, but they couldn't see how to make it happen. The blog brought together a community of people around the world who believed that we had to adopt a positive, proactive, solutions-focused, bottom-up approach. From here, things went very quickly: people started to work together, and one year later, Transition Town Totnes was formally launched.

A few former students in Kinsale had continued to work on the idea of making the *Energy Descent Action Plan* a reality. The town council supported them and gave them a small amount of money. They were the ones who came up with the term "Transition Town."

LA: What did you do first to get Transition started in Totnes?

RH: I must say that this town was—and still is—a particularly productive and suitable community for launching an initiative like Transition. People here have always been looking for alternatives, and its relatively small size (8,500 people) is also an advantage. Food autonomy, for example, has been an issue in Totnes for many years: the UK's first vegetable box scheme emerged here. It was home to the first LETS scheme in the UK (an early experiment in alternative currencies). Plus, Schumacher College, just a few miles away, has also contributed a lot. This avant-garde college teaches its students all the skills necessary for those who want to build a more ecological, humane world that can adapt to the current environmental challenges. More broadly, Totnes has a long history of being a kind of laboratory town. There are five or six places in the UK, like Hebden Bridge, Lewes, and a few others, that play this role. From the outside, people have viewed them as alternative towns, full of hippies. That may sometimes be true, but they also have a great deal of freedom, as the community is very tolerant, and the towns are far enough away from London (Totnes is just over 200 miles from the capital) to be able to create their own identities, their own cultures. People here understood the ideas of local economies and local food more quickly than in many other places.

When I moved to this town, in September 2005, I had just spent ten years in Ireland and didn't know anyone, except for the few friends who had convinced me to come to Devon. I met Naresh Giangrand in a pub; he was very involved in raising awareness about peak oil, which was unusual at the time. I gave him a copy of the Kinsale report, and we started meeting regularly, discussing this classroom assignment that hadn't really involved much interaction with the community. We started a very informal campaign: we showed films, gave small conferences to which we invited local organizations that were sympathetic to our issues, and networked with everyone we knew. I started an evening class, called "Skilling Up for Powerdown," about the skills necessary for a post-carbon world. Many of the people who are still active in Transition took that class.

LA: Raising awareness about the environment and proposing solutions is one thing; motivating people to act is something else. How did you go about it? How did you meet and mobilize the people of Totnes?

RH: The impetus didn't come only from us: after a few months, people would stop us in the street and say: "OK, we understand all the peak oil stuff, now what are we going to do? What's the next step?" So we designed a four-month program, running from September to December 2006. The goal was to launch Transition and to get three or four working groups started, on food, transportation, energy, and housing. We organized a first big evening on food, then ran an Open Space event on the food issue. We then did the same thing concerning energy: an evening, then an Open Space that created a working group—and so on with our main issues. That's how Transition Town Totnes was born.

LA: This plan and these meetings, structured around different themes, were all words, a project, but did not yet involve specific action.

RH: Exactly, these get-togethers were not like ordinary meetings. These were Open Space events where the people who come are already ready to act rather than listen: they are self-organized by the participants, who follow a very effective method. It was developed in the 1990s in America. It's based on the observation that all the best conversations and most productive time in any con-ference take place during coffee breaks. The guy who developed it said: "What would it look like if we designed something that was a day-long coffee break?" The idea of Open Space is that people come together around a question and they self-organize, they run the event themselves. It's very different from a consultation, where people are asked to express what they think someone else ought to do. Open Space offers a venue where people bring what they're passionate about, and they formulate the question that they want to ask or they want to address. There is a lovely kind of freedom in it.

We used this method in Totnes to organize big Open Space events. The first one was on food. The framing question was: "How will Totnes feed itself when cheap energy is gone?" Once the question was raised, we put a timetable up on the wall. People wrote their own questions on post-its, which were then arranged into differ-ent conversations, by subject. Within fifteen minutes, we had the whole timetable for the day, drawn entirely from people's interests and with the subject of each conversation. The only obligation was that if you posted a question, you had to host that conversation and make sure to takes notes of the discussions. It's a very free and open self-organized method. Open Space events can be scary if you're a control freak, because you have to give up control very quickly. The people of Totnes soon realized that this was their proj-ect and that they could achieve their own initiatives. They brought ideas they were passionate about, what they could share with other people: create a shared garden, organize a short supply chain for a certain ingredient, create a purchasing collective, and so on. Or say, for example, that there's a piece of land near your house and every day you walk past it and think: "Somebody should make a food garden on that space." Or at an Open Space event, you ask: "Does someone want to create a vegetable garden here?" You immedi-ately connect with people who need the land. It's an extremely efficient facilitating tool. When I look at the notes taken during these 2007 Open Space events, I see that most of the projects have been launched.

The people who met to discuss a project implemented it together. We created a food group that has been running since 2006, including some of the original members, and others who come and go. Projects are still emerging and are supported by the food group. Immediately after this Open Space event, for example, one of the first initiatives was to plant fruit trees. Starting in 2007, the entire group got together and we planted walnut and almond trees, first on Vire Island, in the middle of the river that runs through town. Since then, we have continued to plant trees: three hundred in all, in the town center as well as on the outskirts. Volunteers in the movement take care of them; they have received training and regularly tend to the trees. Seventy percent of the trees have survived bad weather, vandalism, and other mishaps, and are now strong and producing incredible fruit and nuts–a positive outcome.

This project is completely in sync with the Incredible Edible movement–who are friends of ours–created the followed year, in 2008. There are now shared gardens, open to all, in cities all over the world. This movement speaks out against the millions spent by towns to maintain park spaces covered with non-edible flowers, at a time when lines continue to get longer for free meals provided by charitable organization. Incredible Edible began in the English town of Todmorden (15,000 residents) and has now spread to 250 communities around the world. The movement appeared in campuses, schools, businesses, small towns, and large cities. They all aim to bring people together in support of a growing, widespread project to reclaim food autonomy. The idea is to use every possible space (empty lots, flowerbeds, containers, rooftops) to grow edible species.[1]

---

1. Pam Warhurst and Joanna Dobson, *Incredible! Plant Veg, Grow a Revolution* (Kibworth Beauchamp: Matador, 2014).

Economic and social benefits
of Transition

LA: How did you convince the townspeople to join this project?
Did some of them hesitate getting involved in initiatives that had
some vague, future goal?

RH: Some of them understood that the impact was immediate: meeting up to discuss initiatives and recreate bonds in the community,
having a good time together. People enjoy the process itself, not just
the results. That said, to illustrate the more specific benefits of our
work, we also showed them, statistics in hand, that this approach
acts as an amazing economic lever: we drew up a document called
the Totnes Local Economic Blueprint,[1] which provides an analysis
of the flow of money in the community. It presents the issues and
offers a plan of action. How much do people spend annually on food,
for example? How much of it goes to local businesses as opposed
to large retail chains? What changes would occur if we promoted
short supply chains? Is the idea of Transition economically viable
when detailed figures are used? This blueprint revealed that every
year, people in Totnes spend 30 million pounds on food, 22 million of which is spent in large supermarkets. If they redirected just
10% of this amount to local businesses, they would inject 2 million pounds every year in the local economy. This is no small sum
for a town of 8,500 residents; it can generate significant change.
Local institutions–the Chamber of Commerce, the Town Council,
for example–were all involved in the creation of the *Blueprint* and all
supported the idea: the figures clearly showed how to build a more
resilient economy. Since then, we have distributed this blueprint to
other towns, counties, and even neighborhoods.

1. *Local Economic Blueprint*, https://reconomycentre.org/home/economic-blueprint/.

LA: The story you tell about Transition Town Totnes is full of cheer and enthusiasm. But often, communities have their local disputes, misunderstandings, and incompatible personalities. All of them have people who hold back projects or, on the other hand, are overinvested and burn out in the end, or even hamper initiatives. How do you manage these issues? How did you deal with this as you launched Transition in Totnes?

RH: Totnes probably has more psychotherapists per square foot than anywhere else in the country. We brought them in early on: "How can you help us?" Early on, we were approached by two brilliant women[1] with a long history in psychology and process work, who suggested that the process we were designing would hugely benefit from also exploring the "inner" aspects of the work. We had been wondering, in relation to the town's therapists, "You deal with post-traumatic stress; how do you see setting up a pre-traumatic counseling? How can we prepare for the experience of the incredible paradigm shift that will happen in the next ten to fifteen years? This process will not be all about excitement and opportunity; we're going to have to grieve for a certain lifestyle, nurture the new while letting go of the old. This is going to be very difficult for a lot of us." Sophy and Hilary developed "Inner Transition," a program within the movement, with the goal of examining the psychological and emotional components that could hinder our approach.[2] We wanted to avoid the mistakes of many NGOs and movements before us whose work was hampered by internal conflicts and overwork. I have met too many activists who have burned out and it's a horrible thing. Very few people realize just how much this commitment can lead to a sort of mental exhaustion. It happens in Transition, just like it happens everywhere else. But we have developed a real

1. Sophy Banks and Hilary Prentice: www.transitionnetwork.org.
2. "Inner Transition Totnes," https://transitionnetwork.org/do-transition/transition-in-action/practical-projects/inner-transition-totnes/.

mindfulness in Transition: it's about being more deeply aware of what's happening within ourselves, the organization, and among the members, and therefore with the initiatives themselves. This issue is extremely important to us, and we have set up practices to deal with it. We now hold regular meetings that deal with what's going on with people, aside from the work itself, to defuse problems and make sure the movement remains a place where people want to come and participate. We alternate between regular "doing" meetings and "being" meetings, which give people a chance to ask, "how's everyone doing?" They create a space for personal expression that I've never seen in other organizations. Plus, everyone who works in the heart of Transition Town Totnes has free mentoring available to them at any time they want. When there are particularly stressful or upsetting moments in the project, they know they can receive this kind of support. In hindsight, the contribution of Inner Transition has made a huge difference. It reduces the risk of burnout and exhaustion. The fact is, the people involved carry a huge weight of other people's expectations on their shoulders. They have to remain optimistic and reassure all those who question the work of Transition. It can be a heavy burden.

They also emphasized the importance of learning the skills for running a meeting. When we began, our meetings were all about enthusiasm and energy, and could seem a bit oppressive. A meeting would barely have begun and we were already gung-ho: "Let's create a new group! Launch that initiative right now!" Then we took a step back and thought about how to run meetings where people would feel like they're being heard, where people would want to return, and which have a real structure. They need to know how to deal with disagreements and how to make decisions, to make time for everyone in the group to get to know each other, and to just enjoy being together. Naomi Klein was right when she said that "if you're going to collapse peoples' world views, you have to stick around to pick up the pieces."[1] I think this is an apt image: one of the most irresponsible things you can do is to show a film about climate change to someone and then leave them in the dark. You must support people who are becoming aware of the problem, give them room to digest the bad news, and then assimilate what will happen in their lives. Transition is not just about solar panels and carrots; we believe that what is happening within ourselves is as important as what's happening all around us. Our way of mobilizing people, of communicating and nourishing the process, or inspiring others to join us—all this is enormously important.

Totnes creates its own currency

LA: There were other projects, in addition to food programs and Inner Transition. For example, you launched an innovative idea: a local currency for Totnes. Can residents print their own money? Can you explain how the Totnes currency project unfolded on the ground?

RH: It's a lot easier to create a currency than you think. A group of motivated people got together and created a unit that would serve as the currency, giving it a name (the Totnes Pound), and setting an exchange rate with the national currency: one Totnes Pound equals one pound sterling. The bill we printed started circulating within a network of businesses and people. Everyone purchased a certain number of bills that they then used to pay for goods in businesses that accepted the local currency. These businesses, in turn, used them to pay their local suppliers. The idea was obviously not to replace the national or European currency, which members still

---

1. "Guardian Live: Naomi Klein, *This Changes Everything*," YouTube video, 1:45:16, October 6, 2014.

use, but to introduce an additional currency, and initially, to raise awareness about the poorly understood issues involved in the use of a currency.

LA: How does this type of money, which is used in parallel with the existing currency, address them?

RH: An economy that uses only a single currency, on a country-wide or even larger scale, is as fragile as a farm that practices mono-culture: if a disease strikes, it spreads like wildfire throughout the entire farm. In the same way, if an economic crisis hits a country, the entire world stumbles, as in 2008. From this viewpoint, the existence of alternative currencies, provided there are enough of them, protects the entire economy, just as biodiversity protects an ecosystem. Aside from this economic standpoint, complementary currencies also convey a different set of ethics. First, they assume that users trust each other and remain united. The currency is more like a system of exchange than a tool for speculation and personal enrichment. It encourages mutual assistance and coop-eration. And second, users know what their money is being used for, which is not the case with a traditional banking system, which uses money to finance industries such as weaponry, nuclear energy, and fossil fuel production. These currencies also naturally support short supply chains and local businesses. In short, they change the focus of the economy, promoting relocalization and cooper-ation. From this standpoint, complementary currencies are more qualitative than quantitative in nature, therefore very different from the traditional system.

LA: It's a very bold project; how did you come up with this idea? How did it all work out, from the beginning to the distribution of this currency?

RH: In late 2006, I walked into a building, here in Totnes, that had housed a bank some two hundred years ago. On the wall was a framed Totnes pound bill dated 1810, handwritten in the most beautiful calligraphy. At that time, the town had its own bank and money. I wondered: "What would happen if we printed others and put them into circulation? Would the Queen come throw stones at my windows? Would I be hauled to prison in London?" To find out, we formed an advisory panel of economists from London. We asked them if we could create our own currency. "No idea," they answered, with a collective shrug. "Do it and see what happens!" Not much of an advisory panel! So we went ahead and did it. On March 7, 2007, we printed and distributed notes that were facsimiles of the older currency. We gave ourselves a three-month trial period. Eighteen businesses immediately adopted it. In May, given the enthusiasm for system, we organized a launch event where we decided to continue and expand this experiment. At the same time, we were able to recruit many new volunteers who were interested in this issue. Notified that the project would go on, the media swarmed into town to find out about the Totnes Pound. We organized a press day on May 31, and journalists, mikes and cameras in hand, flocked to the local stores and cafés to cover the story of this currency. The BBC, the *Daily Mirror*, and the *Buenos Aires Herald* were among the media that came. We also organized a conference at Schumacher College[1] with the economist Bernard Lietaer, who has written multiple books and is well-known for his essays on a post-development world (he runs the Wuppertal Institute for Climate, Environment and Energy). The room was packed. He projected so much enthusiasm that once I got back home I couldn't sleep: I could see the incredible potential of this new currency and my mind was racing.

1. This college near Totnes has a holistic approach to learning and teaches the skills needed to construct a more ecological, social world to face current environmental challenges.

LA: And after this successful launch, has this currency remained widely used in the medium- and long-term?

RH: To be honest, the Totnes Pound lost momentum after a few years. We now know the reasons for this slump. We only had one-pound bills, which considerably limited our expansion. Participants needed to have a larger choice of bigger bills. Plus, we didn't pay much attention to how the notes looked and the symbolism that they could embody. To put it bluntly, the artwork was bland and unattractive. For all these reasons, after a while, people talked less and less about this currency, and it started to stall. A second launch was necessary to update the Totnes Pound, to remind people that it still existed, and to attract new users.

Meanwhile, several other towns had learned about our money and decided to launch their own independent currencies. Lewes took the first step, then Brixton issued its own currency (with a portrait of David Bowie on their £10 note!). Right after, Bristol printed its own bills (with the equivalent of 2 million pounds sterling currently in circulation), and did something extraordinary: allowing local taxes and public transportation to be paid in Bristol Pounds. Exeter and Cardiff have also joined in. In short, it's become much more widely accepted. In Plymouth, for example, the programs of half the candidates running for the last municipal elections included the creation of a local currency. Each town has made improvements, and all of them freely exchange their methods and innovations within an association than has brought together the country's local currencies: the Independent Money Alliance.[1]

This idea is gaining broad acceptance, and yet if you look at its development, you see that someone, somewhere, launched a seemingly marginal, even harebrained scheme; it gained traction and reached a tipping point, at which several towns decided to opt in

1. Independent Money Alliance, http://independentmoney.org.uk.

as well. This story shows just how effective it is to launch innovative and relatively small initiatives. They have a considerable capacity to change the course of events, much more than all the talk in the world. Transition's ability to launch this type of idea, starting from scratch, is extremely powerful.

LA: Coming back to Totnes, how did you incorporate the improvements made by other towns?

RH: We had been thinking about relaunching our currency for several years, without actually doing it. We took a long time preparing for this fresh start, drawing on all the good ideas implemented by larger towns. Once we were ready, in May 2014, we issued new bills, along with a whole array of solutions and communication tools. First, we made sure to create beautifully designed, captivating bills—featuring celebrities from Totnes—with attractive colors and original ideas: for example, we have a 21-pound Totnes note. We also issued several denominations (one, five, ten, and twenty-one Totnes Pound notes), so that they're easier for people to use, especially for major purchases. The new bills also have some of the security features of traditional money: watermarks, holograms (a 3D illustration to prevent counterfeiting), engraved silver foil, serial numbers, and so on. The Transition group and its partners also set up an online banking and payment system, as well as mobile phone payment, via text messages. Bristol provided us with the technology that they had already perfected, and most businesses that accept the local currency use these systems. We also created a website,[1] sales outlets, a brochure, and stickers that members can post in their windows.

Building from the experience of other towns perfectly demonstrates the ripple effect of our movement's philosophy: everyone could see the advantages of helping each other within Transition,

1. Totnes Pound, http://www.totnespound.org.

not just in a theoretical way, but through a shared experience. Other Transition Initiatives take an idea that originated elsewhere and improve it; this idea then returns to the place it started, coming full circle. They also realized the impact of their own actions. Incidentally, our town continues to be an incubator, where we test out new projects. Some are picked up elsewhere, others aren't.

LA: Was this new start successful? What's happening with the Totnes Pound?

RH: Today, 140 companies accept it, and the equivalent of 16,000 pounds is now in circulation. The Totnes Pound is still active, but not used as much as it could be. However, it has certainly become a great promotion for Transition Town Totnes, and for the town more widely. Local entrepreneurs spontaneously talk about their attachment to the Totnes Pound, and elsewhere in the UK, we are often identified as "the town that prints its own money." It has become our mascot, a banner behind which we can all rally.

Reassure local authorities and get them involved

LA: You described the way you raised awareness among the people of Totnes and then got them involved in food and monetary issues, but how did you get the elected officials involved?

RH: Our good relationship with the elected officials of Totnes is primarily due to the language that we choose and the way we present our initiatives. We explained the economic benefits for the area and for the local population in a very simple way, to get officials involved as quickly as possible. We drew up the *Totnes Local Economic Blueprint* in partnership with the town council, the District Council, and the Chamber of Commerce. It was a detailed map of the local economy and the flow of money: how much do we each spend on food every year? What proportion of it is spent in large supermarkets? What proportion with local producers? How many jobs would be created if we relocalized our energy production? All the major local institutions participated enthusiastically. This positive way of presenting our projects was decisive: if, for example, we had talked about degrowth, a lot of people would have been put off by the project. By opting instead to talk about new opportunities for local businesses and building a more resilient local economy, people were drawn to it. This issue of language is important because it helps us bring people together. To get the maximum number of people involved and to make Transition a large-scale movement you have to learn to speak a language that can reach everyone. In France, I often answer questions about the relationship between Transition and degrowth. These two themes obviously overlap, but it's not always a good idea to link them, as this concept can be more divisive than unifying.

LA: You may have had open-minded officials, willing to listen, but objectively, your project is disruptive to local politics, isn't it?

RH: Transition is a highly effective tool: it's one of the best ways for citizens to express themselves. Yet it remains unequivocally and resolutely apolitical. Unfortunately, there are people involved in both a political party and a local group who say, "Finally, Transition is pushing my candidate's program." It can be confusing. The conviction motivating their political views and the values inspiring their participation in Transition may be the same. But our approach can only function if it remains distinct from political parties. It's essential, and we constantly repeat this to avoid any confusion. We are very careful about this, and we have noticed that the movement often includes people who belong to a wide cross-section of different parties. In our Totnes group, some members are Conservative, some socialist, some Green, etc. Some—Conservatives and Greens— have even recently added to their tracts that they support one of our projects. We were a bit uneasy with their messaging and responded: "Yes, and well, thanks for your support, we appreciate it a lot, but we like everyone the same here, regardless of their political opinions." In short, we don't want these messages to harm us or create a false image. Everyone should feel at home in Transition.

In any event, when a group like the one in Totnes starts up, it's crucial to develop a good relationship with the local town council. Yet it's best not to rush things: if a group has only existed for three months and hasn't done anything other than show a film or organize a meal, it's better not to speak out too soon. But if a group has already started a shared garden, or is working in the schools, creating a currency, or has formed an energy co-op, then that's the time to go see the mayor, who will already know about the ongoing projects and could probably offer some help. If the relationship is solid and productive, the results can be excellent.

One thing sets us apart from many politicians: we do not have an opinion or a program for everything. Quite the opposite: we like to say that our initiatives and ideas have their limits, and can even be contradictory. In some areas, we don't have any solutions to propose, and having divergent opinions and people pushing in different directions is part of how we work. Our approach, which focuses on positive solutions rather than activism, can therefore generate conflicting views. When a British coffeehouse chain, Costa (the second largest in the world, after Starbucks), tried to open an outlet in Totnes, it was not necessarily Transition's role to get involved in the dispute. Some members weren't comfortable with this. But when the resilience of the local economy is threatened, others necessarily feel concerned, even more so as members of

Transition. This issue also comes up with Transitioners who stand for local elections. But in all these situations, we never say: "No, it's like this and no other way!" I think that this deliberate uncertainty on certain issues is an important asset. We are merely noting the existence of these limits. The tension created is actually a good source of energy.

Empowering residents

LA: How did people, local officials, and politics in general change? How has Transition impacted local politics?

RH: In Totnes, Transition is good for democracy in many ways. Take the anti-Costa campaign, for example. Totnes is one of the very few towns of its size in the UK without a coffee chain store. But our small businesses are vibrant; we have forty independent places where you can buy a cup of coffee. Costa wanted to open a big coffee place at the start of our main street, where all the tourists arrive. Local businesses were worried that their cafés would close, so we ran a big campaign for about that a year and a half. And it worked; we are one of the only places where Costa finally gave up. This boosted confidence: people saw that they could have a real impact on the fate of their communities. This creates what we call "levels of possibility." Over time, these multiple layers of confidence, added one atop another, form a strong foundation on which resilience projects can be built. Unfortunately, in many places, people can't even imagine that they have a voice, simply because they haven't had this past, this story, this experience. Transition is a beautiful way to boost confidence in local areas.

Although it's not a Transition project, I'm also one of the directors of a great community-led development project, Atmos Totnes, which is a more recent example of how people can reengage in the democratic process. It was made possible through a new law, introduced in 2012, called the "Community Right to Build" order. It gives a community the right to decide what to do with a site it owns. To get planning permission, you need to have good local participation and you're required to draw up a master plan for the site, which is submitted to a referendum. During the vote in November 2016, 85.7% of voters approved the community's Atmos development plans. It's a new route to planning permission for community-led projects.

LA: Could you describe this project in more detail?

RH: It began in 2007: a small milk-processing factory that employed 160 people had closed down. We launched a campaign: our goal was to get the community involved, even to the point of purchasing the site. This would create a showcase for a community-led approach to development as a practical, functioning exemplar. We called it "The heart of a new economy." We mobilized a lot of people, promoting the idea that together, we could do something extraordinary. In August 2014, we signed a contract with the site's owners to move the project forward.

People told us that they wanted inexpensive houses built from local, ecological materials that could cut their heating costs as much as possible. They also wanted to participate in the construction process, or at least know the workers who were putting up their homes. When you involve future residents from the very start of the process, you have a better chance of meeting their needs. This project demonstrates that a community can take charge of its own planning, and determine its future rather than letting other people do it for them.

LA: Specifically, how did you proceed? What are the tangible goals of this project?

RH: The community has become its own developer for this 8-acre lot, and the people decide what to do with the land, via referendum. This project creates significant impetus for relocalization: we hope that a high percentage of the construction materials will be sourced locally. In major construction projects, 50% of the budget generally goes toward materials, and developers most often purchase those materials from the global marketplace. We chose to use this expenditure instead as a financial tool to regenerate the local economy. But that's not all: we are going to use local labor (giving training, if necessary) and create small companies that can use this project to get up and running.

Transition links together citizen's initiatives

LA: After several years in existence, Transition Town Totnes has developed projects in various sectors. How are these initiatives interacting now? What synergies have they created? How, for example, has the creation of a local currency helped to set up short food supply chains?

RH: For me, that's really the most important and exciting aspect of Transition: it's the glue that holds all those things together, the narrative that creates coherency. Local currency schemes, local food projects, and renewable energy projects may all exist, but Transition gives it a meaning, shows how they're all part of a larger picture. Take a specific example: Holly Tiffin, a local woman, just started a business called Grown in Totnes. She mills locally grown oats, and has revived an old mill. She presented this project to the Local Entrepreneur Forum, an annual event bringing together local businesspeople. The idea is to help them create a network and to form links among the various elements of Transition. Many residents provided human resources and financial support to the mill and the owner, which gave her a needed boost in confidence. The rather wonderful local New Lion Brewery, of which I am also one of the founding directors, offered to use her oats to make their Totnes artisanal beer. So that this year, we can drink beer made from her grains. But that's not all: the brewery and other customers use our local currency to pay her company. When Transitioners create a project, they immediately think about how they can link it to existing initiatives. Making these connections happen is one of our priorities.

The example of Bristol also demonstrates the synergies of Transition, notably between businesses and local institutions. In this city, where 850 companies accept the complementary currency they created, the mayor's office is now thinking about how the Bristol Pound can help direct spending to businesses that have more local involvement. Every year, the city council spends several million pounds purchasing goods and services for the community. They are considering making the use of the local currency a selection criteria for the bids they receive. This significantly increased the flow of Bristol Pounds, and when the amount of currency exchanged grows larger and larger, the impact is something incredible.

LA: How has Transition evolved in Totnes in recent years? Have new programs, new ideas appeared?

RH: Yes, entrepreneurship has taken on a prominence that I would never have imagined at the start, thanks to our REconomy program, which has existed since 2009. It provides help and a network for people who want to create a business that's compatible with the goals of Transition. It all started when I was researching material for my book *The Transition Companion*.[1] I talked to various people to find out how things were going at this stage in the movement's development. Many of them were in the middle of creating interesting businesses. But as soon as the topic of money came up, people got uncomfortable: environmental activists often seems to think that everything should be voluntary, and money is often viewed as poisoned, immoral, unclean. I discovered this when I was working in permaculture: the idea of making an income was viewed with suspicion. The most ethical approach is supposedly to do everything without money. This bias is extremely detrimental to activism. It fosters what I call a "tyranny of volunteerism," and only attracts people who can give their time for free: generally middle-class people who have enough financial security and skills to get involved.

We therefore shifted our narrative from "we're about local resilience" to "we're about economic resilience, and about creating new livelihoods, and creating a new economy in this town." We organize an annual event in Totnes called the Local Entrepreneur Forum, a real departure from the norm that draws a crowd. A handful of people come and present their projects, while others provide support, either through investments or simply by offering to help with various aspects, such as accounting, the loan of a patch of land, networking with interested parties, and so no. Many people who never participated in any activist movement have joined in. Before, they would never had taken the first step. Before these forums, they used to sit back and say: "Hmm, interesting, but ..." This change in the narrative was decisive.

1. Rob Hopkins, *The Transition Companion. Making Your Community More Resilient in Uncertain Times* (White River Junction: Chelsea Green Publishing Company, 2011).

Local investors in local economies

LA: Can you tell us about one of these forums? What happens?

RH: The idea is to put the entrepreneurs of this new economy in the same room as people who can help them, to discuss projects together. In general, five or so people pitch their business plans, state what their needs are, then take questions. Community members pledge various degrees of support. The main idea is that anyone in the community can become an investor or a promoter in this type of economy: if you lend someone a pen, if you're helping out with the accounting, if you're watching someone's kids, or if you lend them 1,000 pounds, all of these are investments that support this new economy. This kind of flexibility generates a lot of cooperation and mutual assistance; it's very powerful. In its second year, four women presented their kitchen garden project, and they needed 1,000 pounds sterling. They came to the Local Entrepreneur Forum[1] and left with 3,500 pounds and thirty people who had pledged to help. Somebody offered to design their website. This is what happens when communities rally behind projects in this new economy.

Beyond the specific support provided by people attending these forums, the confidence it builds among the project-holders is even more important. When you start a business, you always wonder: "Is this a good idea? Who can I ask to know if it is?" People get so much self-confidence when they stand up in front of three hundred people, introduce themselves, and explain their project. Listening to other people's opinions is also highly motivating. The feedback from project-holders after these forums often bolsters this human aspect. It's the only event I've been to about supporting new businesses that regularly moves people to tears. In a good way.

1. Rob Hopkins: Imagination Taking Power, https://www.robhopkins.net/2017/05/15/places-of-possibility-1-the-totnes-local-entrepreneur-forum/.

LA: What are the criteria for projects presented at these forums?

RH: Six main principles underpin REconomy: ensuring that the economic activity is localized and benefits the community; improving resilience; supporting low-carbon businesses; recognizing that we live in a world with limits, and not working purely for personal profit, but for a wider social purpose; and when possible, bringing assets back into community ownership. Ideally, there's also a commitment to act as part of a web of relationships with other people doing the same thing, rather than everyone working on their own.

LA: How is this approach different in terms of environmental activism?

RH: Activists sometimes tend to think that to change the world they must change other people and their ideas. "Other people will clearly be able to see that we're right," they think. "So, everyone else should change, and if nothing happens, it's because they don't understand." Transition, and specifically the REconomy program says instead: "No—**we** have to change!" We're clearly not looking for profit above all else, but still, let's learn how to talk about money, create a new vocabulary, create ways to meet our needs, develop a different way of looking at the world. If we want to reach the widest possible audience, let's be aware that our ideas are also conveyed by who we are, what our posters look like, and even how we dress. There's no point targeting people who don't share our values; we need to learn to speak their language, to be better understood. I had a conversation with Michael Shuman, an expert on local economies. I asked him: "How can Transition groups radically change local economies?" And he answered: "Go to business school." He was right, and if we want all this to be successful, we need to step up and find inclusive language that can rally lots of people around these ideas.

The REconomy program—and this more benevolent view of money issues—can also attract people who have fewer resources. In Richmond, California, I met an activist named Doria Robinson, who works in a very poor, mostly black community, training people in urban agriculture. When I talked about encouraging entrepreneurship so that people could create livelihoods and jobs and about the "tyranny of volunteerism," she answered: "It's so great to hear somebody say that. In my community, if this revolution depends on volunteers, I can't be a part of it, nor can most of the people where I live." When I visit Transition groups who ask me how to bring in new people or engage younger people, or make our group more diverse, I tell them that our REconomy program is the response to many of these questions. It provides a way for people who don't usually participate to get involved in Transition.

Personal convictions in a professional world: it's possible!

LA: Do some people have two separate lives: a private one, with concerns for solidarity and ecology, and a professional one that inhibits their personal sensibilities?

RH: Yes, I was recently asked to speak at a major computer company. Many people in the company are also involved in the movement. They are active in Transition in their communities, but when they go to work at this company, they leave all that at the door. They say that their work place is interested in their brains, not their hearts, which they leave at home. But a place of work can fully integrate both the culture of Transition and the heart.

LA: How to resolve this duality? Including these issues in the professional sphere could be intimidating or even frightening in certain contexts.

RH: Sometimes it's about starting with very small things, which lead to others. For example, employees could transform their work places so that they are no longer in bleak industrial zones, with fairly pointless decorative plants, but a place where, when you arrive there's a beautiful vegetable garden, and the staff work on it during lunch, if they want. This small initiative creates a place where people can exchange ideas, where subjects come up spontaneously. It then becomes a presence, a permanent showcase for Transition in the company. A positive action like this–or setting up a carpool plan, for example–shifts the dialogue so that it can be heard by the entire staff. This approach can be developed further with a view to integrating the process into the company's operational practices, by encouraging a business to source its materials locally, etc.

For some people, bringing Transition into a company is a bold move. But it's essential, if only to remain true to our own selves. Taking this step helps to extend the movement to diverse social strata and to broader economic sectors. This also contributes widely to the expansion of Transition.

2

TOTNES GOES VIRAL

A ripple effect

LA: A few years back, you were just an ordinary citizen without any particular profile. How do you explain the enthusiasm for your initiatives and the fact that 1,400 Transition Initiatives now exist?

RH: We did not plan it out: we had dreamed of this type of outcome, it's true, but it's not something we had anticipated, or even less, worked toward. I think that if you have a good idea, if it's effective, it spreads itself. The viral aspect of Transition is part of its basic structure; it develops spontaneously. When Transition started in Brazil, for example, it wasn't because of a specific project: it wasn't like a Coca-Cola executive saying: "Brazil is ours: let's open an office there tomorrow!" No, it was people in Brazil who thought it was an interesting idea and pursued it on their own.

LA: Yes, but you didn't even try to promote your initiatives through mainstream media. How did people in countries as far away as Japan, Brazil, and the US discover you?

RH: Transition has spread in amazing ways. One day, in 2007–so this was at the start of the movement–I received a link to a You-Tube video. It showed a woman in New Zealand giving a talk in her town. I had never spoken to her, and there was no book yet out at that point. She gave a fantastic presentation about Transition, perfectly clear and incredibly effective. In short, Transition could not have happened before the Internet, before YouTube, before blogs. This technology contributed enormously to our growth. That same year, a Mexican journalist called to interview me about Transition Town Totnes. When his article came out, we translated it for the people in the town. In it, he made an analogy with John Lennon's song "Imagine," and included a map of the UK which showed just three places, London, Liverpool ... and Totnes! That gave people in Totnes a good laugh!

In April 2009, there was a course at Schumacher College called "Life After Oil." One of the participants, Ben Brangwyn, really opened my eyes. He came up to me and said: "You look like a man standing under a tsunami. You need a network to support what you're doing." He was right: interest in Transition was growing all around the world, and it was just Naresh and me in front of our computers answering all the emails. We had to set up an organization to manage and support this development. He told me: "I'll give you a year of my time, free, to work on all this." Four months later, we had found funding to create a proper structure. That's when we wrote a document about how we wanted this network to be. We didn't want to be a formal membership organization, where people pay ten pounds a year and receive newsletters in exchange. We simply wanted something to have we could pass along, so that everyone could take it and adapt it to their own situation.

A practical, accessible tool for everyone

LA: So how would you describe the practical tools you developed? If I wanted to start a Transition group, what should I do?

RH: The first thing is to contact other Transition groups nearby, by checking out Transition websites.[1] Transition Network created a free guide called *The Essential Guide to Doing Transition*, which is the best place to start. Then I would suggest trying to find other people who might be interested, and get them together for an event, whether you show a film on post-oil

1. Transition United States, http://www.transitionus.org/.

alternatives or just organize a meal. Once you get these people together, always keep questioning yourself: "Who else should be here? Who have we forgotten. Who else should we invite?" From here, create an initiating group to get things rolling, people who may not necessarily expect to still be involved in a few years' time. Their role is to lay the foundations for the Transition group so that people who come along later can easily step in and carry on with the work. You create a website, open a bank account, form an organization–these are all the first things to do.

A key aspect to creating a group that's perceived as effective is its ability to do something practical at the earliest stages: organize a local produce market, schedule a bike repair day, put on a festival. You can't just spend months sitting around talking, you have to do something. One you've had a successful first initiative, I recommend that Transitioners celebrate their accomplishments from the very start; it's more important than you think. The meetings of environmental NGOs tend to be very solemn affairs, so much so that when they achieve something, they're too busy running on to the next thing and too serious to celebrate their successes. Instead of constantly pushing forward, it's important to stop, look at what's been done and say, "Well done everyone, that was fantastic!"

It's also important to create links with other organizations to form a network and close relationships with other partners. It makes a difference to feel that you're part of a much larger movement. Belonging to a network that includes all the Transition initiatives is a considerable asset; whether it's in a small town, an urban neighborhood, or elsewhere, the group belongs to a huge learning network that now has over ten years of experience. We have acquired solid expertise and can suggest multiple tools as well as two-day workshops all about how to most effectively launch a group. There are good training programs in the States, with

American trainers. Ideally, you would invite eight to ten motivated people, and bring in a trainer rather than send two people
from a group to a training session in Totnes, who would have
to remember it all and bring it back to the group. It can also be
interesting to invite other Transitioners in your area to give talks
about what they're doing.

LA: Your methods have a little extra touch of fun and lightheated-
ness. Where does this come from?

RH: Everyone learning about our tools soon sees that they're easy
to pick up. The movement's optimism should also manifest through
a sense of humor and equanimity. People who learn about Transition realize that they don't have to pore through a whole batch of
boring texts to get involved. It's all here, easily accessible–which
doesn't prevent those who want to pursue something further from
finding the resources they need. We recently created "The Essential Guide to Doing Transition," which many people find very
useful. It offers what we call the "7 Essential Ingredients of Transition," which we've distilled over the years of doing this as the
key things you need to think of in order to get started where you
like. The first is Healthy Groups, which stresses the importance
of focusing as much on how a group works, as on what it does:
that a good group culture, mutual support, and learning to work
well together, all really matter. The second, Vision, stresses the
importance of imagining the future you want to create in advance
of taking steps towards it. The third, Involvement, offers tools for
inviting your community to get involved in what you are doing,
as the depth and diversity of relationships our groups create is
one of the key indicators of their success. The fourth, Networks
and Partnerships, explores why it matters that we collaborate and
work with other groups, and that the skillful building of partnerships and collaboration will really help projects to flourish. The

fifth Essential Ingredient is Practical Projects, that it really matters that people do things, create visible manifestations, rather than just talking. And that those projects are eye-catching, playful, impactful, and inviting. The sixth is Part of a Movement, where we invite people to connect to the wider movement, to share their stories, their successes and failures. And the final one is Reflect and Celebrate. All too often in activist circles, we see a model where people work hard, then burn out, then work hard, then burn out again. One of the reasons is that we rarely stop to celebrate, to appreciate each other, to reflect on what worked well and what we could improve upon. We suggest that every meeting, every event, every project, should include elements of reflection and celebration. When put together, these ingredients have shown themselves to really increase the chances of groups being successful in getting established.

LA: You also talk about "The 7 Buts"?

"THE 7 BUTS"
This is a list of the pretexts that people use, consciously or not, to avoid getting involved in a project that implies radical change.

1/ "BUT ... we've got no funding"

This is not really an issue. Funding is a very poor substitute for enthusiasm and community involvement, both of which will take you through the first phase of your Transition.

Funders can also demand a measure of control, and may even steer an initiative in directions that run counter to community interests. You will reach a point where you have specific projects that will require funding, but until that point, you'll manage. Retain power over your initiative and don't let a lack of funding stop you.

2/ "BUT ... they won't let us"

Some people fear that any ambitious initiative will automatically be attacked by faceless bureaucrats or corporations; in short, those in power. Don't get held back by imaginary opponents, especially as Transition Initiatives operate below the radar, without making either victims or enemies. So far, they haven't incurred the wrath of any existing institutions. On the contrary, you will be surprised at how many people in positions of power will be enthused and inspired by what you are doing. Many businesses are already pursuing and supporting sustainable development, and are well aware of climate change issues. They will help, rather than hinder, your efforts.

3/ "BUT ... there are already active green groups in this town"

You'd be very unlucky to encounter any "eco-turf wars." What your Transition Initiative will do is form a common goal and sense of purpose among the existing groups. Some of them will likely appreciate the new vigor you bring. Liaising with a network of existing groups toward an Energy Descent Action Plan will enhance and focus their work, rather than replicate or supersede it. Expect them to become your allies, which is crucial to the success of your Transition process.

4/ "BUT ... no one in this town cares about the environment anyway"

One could easily be forgiven for thinking this, given the seemingly apathetic consumer culture in which we live. But scratch a bit deeper, and you'll find that people are already passionate about many Transition initiatives. The key is to go to them, rather than expecting them to come to you.

5/ "BUT ... surely it's too late to do anything"

It may be too late, but the likelihood is that it isn't. Which means that endeavors by you (and others) are crucial. Don't let hopelessness sabotage your efforts. As Vandana Shiva says: "The uncertainty of our times is no reason to be certain about hopelessness."[1]

---

1. Vandana Shiva was speaking at the 2007 Soil Association Conference in Cardiff, Wales.

6/ "BUT ... I don't have the right qualifications"

If you don't do this, who else will? It doesn't matter that you don't have a PhD in energy efficiency, or years of experience in gardening. What's important is that you care about where you live, that you see the need to act, and that you are open to new ways of engaging people. Useful qualities for someone starting a Transition Initiative include: a positive attitude, being friendly, and basic knowledge of the place and of a few key people in the locale.

7/ "BUT ... I don't have the energy for doing that!"

There is a quote that's often ascribed to Goethe: "Whatever you can do or dream you can, begin it. Boldness has genius, power, and magic in it."[1] The experience of beginning a Transition Initiative certainly shows this to be the case. While the idea of preparing your town or city for life beyond oil may seem staggering in its implications, there is something about the energy unleashed by this process that is unstoppable. Making the leap from "Why is no one doing anything" to "Let's do something" generates sufficient energy to keep it moving. Indeed, many people will come forward to help.

RH: This list describes the seven hesitations and fears that are most often expressed by people skeptical of the movement: "But we don't have the money, the people in this town are not interested in the environment, but other green initiatives already exist, and so on." This is what relatively unmotivated people add, just after saying: "Yes, yes, it's a great idea, but ..." When you hear this type of phrase, subsequent projects don't get off the ground. Others talk about a more or less imaginary external enemy: "Once the project starts to work, 'they' will prevent us from moving forward." But this very rarely happens, because the men and women

1. For a detailed discussion of the genealogy of this quote, see "Popular Quotes: Commitment," The Goethe Society of North America, March 5, 1998: http://www.goethesociety.org/pages/quotescom.html.

who work in institutions are quite simply men and women who would like Transition to be successful. The purpose of this tool is to try to identify the fear and obstacles that often produced in the mind, and to overcome them.

The "do-it-yourself" culture

LA: These tools are freely available, so that everyone can draw on the principles of Transition and adapt them as needed. Is this broad freedom to act one of the keys to the movement's success?

RH: Yes, it's been a decisive factor in its development. For an idea to spread, it should be easily appropriated by everyone. We therefore provide tools to help local groups; the only requirement is that they share their own experiences with the rest of the movement. We have drawn up a very simple list of values and principles to be applied–it's all that's needed to belong to Transition. In reality, we're a learning network. We clearly determine what is Transition and what isn't, before we tell people to "take all this and create your own project." Yet ultimately, we are conducting an experiment: no one has all the knowledge or can say exactly how to proceed. This is the basis of Transition's success. It gives the impression that the movement developed on its own, effortlessly, but that's really an illusion: we did a lot of groundwork to spread this information, first with our neighbors, then via the blog, film screenings, and so on. In fact, that's my role in Transition: to motivate people by talking about the most interesting projects, thereby inspiring new ones. I'm a storyteller really.

A couple of years ago, I went to London to give a presentation to an organization that supports the social economy. The participants at this kind of event are successful businesspeople who support the idea of giving back to society by backing social economy initiatives. Project-holders give a fifteen-minute presentation and then answer questions. If they like what you do, they'll help you in different ways. I was therefore invited to their conference. After my presentation, instead of questions, there was a long silence. Then a man said, with a touch of irony: "What you have done is to create a very powerful brand, an internationally recognizable brand, and you're giving it away for free to people all over the world, over whom you have no control whatsoever. You're completely mad!" And I answered: "But it works."

The movement was never meant to be a huge machine: the Transition Network today employs eleven people, including me, and I think twenty would be the maximum. If we ended up with two hundred people, I think something would have gone wrong. We now have thirty-four national "Hub" organizations, some of which have paid staff. Not many organizations spend so much time trying to give away power that they could keep. It's usually the opposite.

LA: What's behind the words used in your movement, like "transition" and "resilience," and why are they so important? Why don't you use "sustainable," a word everyone knows?

RH: Sustainable development implies that by consuming in a different way, everyone on earth could have a sustainable lifestyle that's compatible with the environment. It suggests that the standard of living in poor countries could match that of wealthy countries, and that we could continue to live on the planet without depleting its resources. But this concept completely ignores the fact that we are going to face crises, or the importance of local economies in this evolution. Thus the importance of assimilating the concept of resilience, which more specifically describes a material that can withstand a shock and then recover its initial characteristics, or the ability of an individual to successfully meet challenges. Even though the word "sustainable" is often horribly misused–notably in the UK, where the government talks about "sustainable growth"–it remains relevant and it is a useful concept, an effective lens through which to look at a situation. It's an idea that encompasses solidarity, democracy, environmental protection, and an entire array of positive values. This is not always the case with the word "resilience." You could, for example, say that North Korea is resilient. Some models may be resilient, while oppressing and denying freedom to their citizens. Resilience alone is not enough; you can have local economies that make people miserable. I see resilience as the missing piece of sustainability, because it then occurs in a context of social justice.

People sometimes ask me: "How do you know that creating more local economies won't end up being worse than that we have now?" I don't think that's possible, exactly because Transition is based on values of social justice, democracy, self-organization, and cooperation. If someone started up an economic resilience initiative that wasn't in sync with this, it couldn't be a part of Transition, it wouldn't click, it would be incompatible. But the word "transition" doesn't always work: it refers to different things in different places, and is sometimes associated with specific historical events in a country, making it hard to use. Some countries with a history of fascism used the phrase Great Transition, and don't want to adopt this term. It doesn't really matter what word is used, as long as the principle remains the same. But the multiple ways it is used says a lot about the flexibility of the concept. In a favela of São Paulo in Brazil, where Transition is happening, people are less concerned about oil and climate change; for them, it's about social justice, anti-violence, empowerment, and the defense of women. Transition adapts to highly diverse contexts.

LA: The open source and selfless aspect of this movement seems to reflect your own personality. What events inspired you to adopt this approach. How did you become this easy-going, reassuring, but radical figure?

RH: The time I spent in a Tibetan Buddhist monastery in Italy, which we discussed earlier, was certainly formative in terms of my concept of responsibility: Buddhism teaches us to first look within before acting, and the idea of sharing power—which fosters a sense of responsibility—results from this idea that everyone joins hands. But even before this period, punk culture had a huge influence on me. The whole "do-it-yourself" slogan sounds like a bit of a cliché, but it comes from the punk movement, and for me, it was decisive. I didn't have colored hair or any real punk style, but I loved the philosophy. Punks were saying: "So you don't like this music? Then make your own! You don't like this label? Make one! You don't like the people in this group? Create your own!" A while ago, I came across a punk fanzine from 1976 that showed how to make music with three chords and said: "Here are three chords, now form a band." I loved that message, that spirit. When I was fourteen, a punk label called Crass Records used to put out essays and printed highly political, compelling messages on their record sleeves. One of their records was about the meat industry, and it make me go vegetarian; I've been one ever since. The punk culture lit a kind of spark inside me. At that point, I started going to antinuclear demonstrations, and marches against the apartheid regime in South Africa. I got very involved in the fight to stop the construction of new roads during the final years of the Thatcher government. Many of these projects were destroying magnificent spots. I then discovered permaculture, which tied all these issues together for me. This method is based on the do-it-yourself culture, but also built on a profound concern for the environment and ecology.

It is also incredibly empowering: you don't need to study soil science for years to know how to make good soil, you can just go ahead and do it; you don't need to study architecture for years to build a straw house—you need to put up the foundations, the roof, and the walls. I love this spirit. It's this empowering spirit to act that inspires me.

Launching hundreds of initiatives

LA: Your movement now has more than a thousand Transition Initiatives; how did most of them start? What were the first initiatives taken in the various communities?

RH: Newly formed groups most often start with issues around food. They may work together on a shared garden, for example, or create small food production businesses, like a CSA, using local grains and labor. In a world where most of our bread is made by supermarket chains, and where independent shops are disappearing from our downtown areas, this is a key element in building a new society. The advantage of the food sector is its simplicity: to produce food, you don't have to ask permission from anyone and you don't need much money. In addition, people who like to grow fruit and vegetables, people who like to cook, also like to share their experiences. We've seen that food projects often lead to other initiatives: food often primes the pump; it's the spark that inspires people to go further. These simple initiatives build confidence among those who launch projects, and it's essential: too many people remain passive because they don't see how their actions could benefit society or the environment. A Transition group in Portugal created a community garden in front of an apartment block, for the residents. They became incredibly motivated, and told me that they hadn't acted before because they couldn't see how their efforts could have any effect on the world's problems. From this viewpoint, the production of fruit and vegetables is a clear, concrete example.

Unfortunately, the initiatives people value the most are large-scale projects. To get visibility, you need to show the most spectacular projects, backed up with significant statistics and data. But I am constantly talking about small projects–like this garden in Portugal–which are just as important as other, more impressive ones, like the Bath & West Community Energy company. The small Portuguese garden has more potential to raise awareness than you'd think. It illustrates the importance of relocalizing food production via short supply chains and the goal of greater autonomy. Food sovereignty on a local level is one of the cornerstones of Transition. These modest initiatives are therefore the stimuli that we need today.

LA: What are the next steps, once the food initiatives have been developed? What are the most common projects among Transition Initiatives?

RH: Some very simple initiatives can be developed, like the one we call Transition Streets: it's about bringing together neighbors, who can share information about saving energy, bulk food purchases, and sharing transportation options (carpooling, car-sharing, shared electric bikes). But often, when a Transition initiative has reached a certain level, after achieving several initiatives, it can also create its own currency or start to look for a self-managed energy supply system. The latter often means creating a cooperative that belongs to the residents who install one or several small-scale energy production systems (for example, solar panels). In this way, residents, companies, and communities can choose the type of energy they produce, protect themselves against energy crises and price increases, and create local jobs. This aspect is also one of the basic stages in the life of a Transition Initiative.

LA: Which communities best represent the Transition approach?

RH: The Bath Community Energy Company, in Somerset, UK, is one of the most exciting. It developed from the Transition Bath and Transition Corsham groups, and devised an investment model where people could invest their pensions in a community energy company. They then became the owners of a local, renewable energy supplier. It's an extremely ambitious project, as they managed to bring in start-up investment from one of the six largest energy companies in the UK: Scottish and Southern Energy. This company agreed to invest 1 million pounds to get the project started. The co-op was therefore able to issue and offer share options, through which people received a return quite early on. A lot of community-owned energy companies are careful to tell their investors: "Buy our shares, invest in us, and maybe at some point in the future we might be able to give you some money." But Bath said from the very beginning that they would pay 6% every year, right from the start. The money invested by Scottish and Southern Energy meant that they could implement some highly visible projects that they could point to when looking for new shareholders, notably the installation of solar panel systems on local schools. They then did a share launch and invited people to invest, raising three-quarters of a million pounds. A lot of people moved their pensions to this project. Last year, they did a second share option, and raised about 2 million pounds again, and the city council invested money as well. They now have a big, successful energy company owned by local citizens. This large-scale project demonstrates the Transition is not merely about creating community gardens or other small projects, but can also encompass a highly ambitious approach that aims to feeds cities, produce their energy, and so on. Faced with this challenge, local people are willing to invest, which is highly promising for the future.

Another example is Transition Brixton, a predominantly poor neighborhood in south London. One of their projects is Brixton Energy, which works with people living in public housing. Solar panels were put on the tops of apartment blocks, and the younger residents, after receiving training, worked alongside the contractors who installed them. Some of the money invested by the people was also used to make the buildings more energy efficient. For the first project, Brixton Solar Energy 1, the investors were primarily more middle-class local people; for the second and third buildings, Brixton Solar Energy 2 and 3, most of the people investing were those who actually lived in these blocks. They contributed between 200 and 300 pounds, because they could see it was a good investment. This means that, despite low income and low savings, they chose to invest the little money they had in this project, rather than place it in a bank. They can see the difference it makes. Brixton is, in places, a poor neighborhood, Bath is a wealthy one, but the idea of Transition works very well in both places.

Transition adapts and cooperates with existing initiatives

LA: Transition is not relevant everywhere: in some neighborhoods and towns, people have already understood that they should get together to relocalize their food and energy supplies. Does this movement target those who are just discovering how to make ecology practical and need a framework to get started?

RH: First of all, what's most important about any project is the actual content, whether these initiatives are called "Transition" or not. That said, some of our groups are working in areas where, prior to Transition, the environment was already a core issue, through multiple projects. But people who joined the movement realized that a larger network brought real advantages. They are happy to be part of a large, global community and to belong to this kind of learning network. Some of our programs, like Inner Transition, can be extremely helpful to them as they pursue their projects, as it supports the group in a long-term way. Similarly, REconomy offers substantial support for broadening the spectrum of people interested in Transition: building a new economy that includes entrepreneurs and creating links with the community adds an extra element to what they have already done, and people notice it.

Some groups of involved citizens, after working for years on initiatives, also need to sharpen their focus concerning their priorities and direction. The Transition group in Bristol was created in 2007. They had a hard time getting started, because there was already so much happening in the city. The first Transitioners felt like they were drawing from the same pool of people who were already involved in lots of other things. They chose to focus on the city council, and to support it by doing brave, interesting things. For example, they wrote the first peak oil report, before any other council in the country, and they also conducted a food resilience study, then introduced the Bristol Pound, which was also a result of their work with the council. Despite all the preexisting initiatives, Transition found its place and has played a significant role in Bristol. In other places with lots of projects, Transition can be a network, the connection between all the initiatives already happening. We can weave all these things together to tell a story that makes sense to lots of groups and organizations. Creating this link among all the people and projects is key to moving forward in environmental efforts.

LA: Is Transition is a catalyst for change?

RH: Yes, exactly. Transition makes people more efficient, more dynamic. At the start, some groups felt that they were just going around and round; they started community gardens and kept doing the same things for years. But when they began to feel connected via the networking of ideas, they were able to go beyond this stage and step up to another level.

I would add that in some situations, people can't grasp the relevance of Transition, even though its contribution can be decisive. London, for example, is a huge city, and many people don't see how agricultural issues—viewed as rural ones—concern them. There's a great project in London called "Growing Communities." It's not a Transition thing, but it has inspired many of us. Its initial mission was to coordinate supplies of local produce for thousands of people. But they provide so much more: they look for local solutions to feed urban populations, and they support people who want to organize to meet their own needs locally. The challenge consists in finding where they can source local supplies in London. Can this capital city be self-sufficient? Growing Communities drew up a diagram consisting of concentric circles of "food zones";[1]–it shows that 2.5% of London's food supply could be grown in the capital's gardens, rooftops, and balconies (the center of the diagram); 5% in a few kitchen gardens in the city (first circle); 17.5% could come from peri-urban areas if we re-create a link with them; and so on. In all, it concludes that 80% of the food supply could be produced locally. This diagram and the project to create an economic model that would relocalize activities is hugely important. They are among the initiatives that help people conceive of a nearly oil-free and emission-free society, one in which they could get involved.

1. "The Food Zones," Growing Communities, https://www.growingcommunities.org/food-zones.

Renewable energies: crucial for change

LA: The process of relocalizing food production and the economy is at the heart of Transition. But you say that it needs to push for replacing fossil fuels with renewables. Why? What's the link between these sectors?

RH: In a world dominated by long supply chains, overconsumption, and widespread waste, even an abundant production of renewable energies will be insufficient to meet demand. The relocalization that our movement promotes, along with reduced consumption, are therefore essential if we are to stop using fossil fuels. Furthermore, the use of renewables offers advantages that many people don't even suspect: as opposed to highly centralized oil or nuclear fuel production, solar, wind, and hydroelectric power can be created with local infrastructure. Communities can therefore manage their own energy through cooperatives, and gain control of decisions as to how to power their homes and companies. By definition, this model is only possible with locally generated resources. For the time being, we get our energy supplies, as well as building materials and food, from extremely powerful companies based far from the communities in which they work.

Another benefit of citizen-run production co-ops is that they encourage energy-saving efforts: the income they generate is not swallowed up by a few shareholders, freeing up funds to insulate more homes in the community, rather than waiting for other forms of financing–government or European–which are slow to come.

Of course, we can't forget that fossil fuels have been a phenomenal and historically unprecedented boost to the modern era. They are the reason we have multiple products that never used to be available in stores. But this economic model, based on cheap oil, has also generated a colossal amount of waste: based entirely on cheap energy, it has not encouraged research into more economical solutions, thereby creating a tremendously inefficient system.

LA: You often talk about the energy, food, and currency initiatives of Transition, but far less about transportation. Yet it is a crucial issue.

RH: Many Transition Initiatives encourage people to ride bikes. Some of them have created free services: every week, a free bike maintenance service is set up on a square. Others also help build confidence among people who are afraid to ride their bikes on city streets. Small groups of Transitioners have also promoted carpooling in their streets and neighborhoods, or obtain subsidies to purchase electric bikes that are shared among a group of people. They take turns keeping them maintained so that those who live in the neighborhood can use them when they like. Aside from these initiatives, we do not have any large-scale projects in this sector.

The power of an ultra-lean organization

LA: Expanding from Totnes to the entire world is a new order of magnitude. How have you financed an expansion to forty-seven countries?

RH: The movement did not expand because of more investment; it was the reverse of how things usually happen for an NGO or a company that wants to grow. Many groups spontaneously appeared around the world, then the Transition Network, which connects all these groups, was created to better coordinate the movement–which then led us to look for funding. More specifically, after two or three years, Transition had spread all over the world, with energy cooperatives, groups involved in food, and others in housing. Everything was growing, presenting a real risk of become fragmented. We had reached a point at which the project needed someone to act as an overall coordinator. If you're not careful, all this energy can be dissipated. It can happen very quickly: after a few years, the initiatives that are created retain only a vague idea of the Transition principles on which they were based, and the message is lost. We call this the "doughnut effect": all the energy moves to the outside, leaving a hole in the middle. To keep the whole thing together, you need to keep the jam in the middle of the doughnut. It's an incredibly difficult thing to get funding for though. Funders tend to either like to support stand-alone projects with a beginning, middle, and end, or a network, like Transition Network. That unglamorous doughnut-filling is something they tend to steer clear of sadly.

LA: Was it difficult to find funding to set up Transition Network?

RH: No, donors generally like to support expanding networks that are spreading ideas. Three weeks after we started Transition Network, we got a call from a foundation in London that wanted to meet with us. "How can we help?" they asked. We were surprised to get this support so easily. We were very lucky. And in fact, they gave us the core funding we needed for the first three years of the Network. They also provided a great deal of support in terms of how we created the organization. Their goal was to help us establish a long-term organization. Their help was extremely useful and valuable to us.

LA: Would more funding help you expand further?

RH: Yes, of course, but not in the same way that it would for, say, a campaigning organization. The idea that throwing more money at something will always have the desired impact is often an illusion: we went to the US for a conference two years ago, an event that brought together the country's biggest philanthropic trusts. Someone asked us: "What would it cost to expand Transition all around the world? It would probably take billions, right?" We answered: "No, more like millions." The unique nature of Transition, and what differentiates it from many other approaches, is its capacity to go viral. The development and effectiveness of many NGOs depend on their funding. We don't operate like that at all. Money can even hinder a movement. For the first two or three years after you launch a local group, you don't need much money. Because you don't have money, you go out into your community, you work hard, you raise awareness, you involve people, you network with people; it creates a powerful foundation on which you can build. Transition can create a sense of possibility, of excitement, of hope, that lots of funded projects just never do. It creates integrity, which is no small thing: people get involved because they love the ideas.

LA: Once the Network is created, are there other stages of development that require funding?

RH: Yes, we have seen that the success of a group depends a great deal on whether they have received training or not. The Transition training team is a major component in our success. But it's not all: it's key to have donors who are ready to provide the initial funding for larger-scale, more high-risk projects. If you want to start an energy cooperative, for example, before issuing share options to residents to start the company, a certain amount of money is necessary to get the first stages of the project going. They will need someone to provide this financing, with the provision that he or she is taking a risk. Once the first installations have been constructed, once the project has really taken off and people trust it, the second stage can begin: funds can come from people in the local community, who can see that the initiative is serious. To sum up, money can play a role in different stages of a group's development: maintaining the overall coherence after an initial launch stage, financing training for new groups, and providing seed money for some of the riskier, larger projects.

In Scotland, the government set up funding for community climate projects, called the Climate Challenge Fund. During our international Transition Conference, people from Scotland told us that they had received government money from this fund to finance their initiatives. At first we were amazed, and jealous: "No way! Really?" Recently, many of them lost their funding; for some, it didn't matter, they remained active. But other groups had been created because they had received funding. They hadn't built the foundations of a group that starts from scratch, without money, organizing film projections, meetings, networking, and events; because they had skipped this stage, they didn't survive.

In some countries, local government institutions have provided financial support to Transition, including the Ministry of Sustainable Development and Infrastructure in Luxembourg and the Belgian government, but you have to be careful and scrupulous: I think it would be more problematic than helpful to give a million pounds to every Transition group in the world, at least in the early stages of their evolution.

LA: Are people attracted to Transition precisely because of the small structure and limited amount of money it generates?

RH: Yes, just look at this office we're sitting in. If you came to do this interview and I was sitting in an enormous glass and steel office in a big leather chair with a cigar, instead of this closet, you'd probably get a different impression.

Transition is more than activism

LA: Initially, the movement was focused on ecological issues; how would you describe it today?

RH: There are now 1,500 groups around the world, including 400 in the UK, with thousands of people involved. We recently brought together representatives from nineteen national groups in Lyon for a four-day conference. We were invited to the US to participate in the Environmental Grantmakers Association conference, and we also toured seven American states to support existing initiatives and to encourage new ones. In addition, we have 150 trainers around the world. Their role is to support the creation of Transition groups and initiatives, or to give them an extra boost and aid those that are already up and running.

This development would not have been possible if the movement was only targeting environmental activists. When I meet with groups, I've noticed that many participants don't have the usual activist profile. Many people who get involved in Transition wouldn't usually campaign for an environmental cause. But is Transition really a form of activism? A lot of people would say no, that they are merely trying to rethink and rebuild the place where they live, no more, no less. They're working to change things for the better, not by global campaigns, but piece by piece, community by community, street by street. You could say this is a very radical activist model for change, or you could say that this is just the way people do things. A lot of the people who get involved don't see themselves as activists at all. In fact, the defining characteristic of Transition is that it's not about a single issue—one that you either agree or disagree with—but deals with questions as diverse as energy, finance, agriculture, and transportation. The multiple subjects we tackle also contribute to this diversity: people who like to plant trees can be useful in a Transition project, as can those who are interested in kitchen gardens, bikes, or renewable energies. Once they are involved in the movement, they may go from one project to another, and discover issues they are less familiar with.

LA: Has the REconomy program spread elsewhere in the world?

RH: After it began in the UK, the REconomy program started up in five other countries. It now exists in eleven countries, including Great Britain, Belgium, Brazil, Croatia, Germany, Italy, Luxembourg, Mexico, and the Netherlands. We also run eleven learning exchange platforms for businesses working on ecology and solidarity-based projects, to help them develop in the best possible way. We help them work with local partners through networking and local councils. We have toured all the ongoing projects in the UK. There are some fascinating ones, like a farm in Norwich, owned by two hundred members,[1] which was able to start up and develop thanks to the forum. It grows food and asks shareholders to participate, including working in the fields. People running REconomy in Totnes and Brixton are now working on a crowdfunding system that would encourage investments in companies that subscribe to the principles of Transition. There are several large projects outside the UK, like a community-run vineyard in Liège (Belgium). This business was created locally and is based on environmental and social criteria, with the goal of involving the greatest number of residents. This cooperative now has 1,200 members, has planted thirty acres of grape vines, and is about to produce 100,000 bottles of wine. By setting a price of 500 euros per share, the business was able to raise 1,850,000 euros. Now that's an exciting, large-scale project! When I asked them how they did it, how they found the confidence for such a big ask, I was

---

1. Norwich Farm Share, http://norwichfarmshare.co.uk.

told: "This is Belgium. People like wine, and they have money. Don't be afraid." Good advice.

With the expansion of the REconomy program, now when we meet decision-makers, whether in the business sector or the administration, we can speak the same, or at least a similar, language. When we explain how money circulates and how it leaves communities, they understand. But this also means that we have to be vigilant: it's not about Richard Branson opening a Transition supermarket. I am also careful about the word "entrepreneur": when government ministers say we need more entrepreneurs, I don't think we're talking about the same thing. This difference in vision also holds true for so-called social entrepreneurs: only 2 to 3% of them understand the key role of localization, and are motivated by climate change. Most of them want to replace services the central government doesn't want to do anymore with a different kind of economic model. While that's vital, and great, it's just a fraction of what it could be. Within ten years' time, I hope that Transition will have created lots of jobs, particularly in sectors like construction, food, and energy.

LA: So you don't view Richard Branson and David Cameron as models. How is your vision different from theirs? You don't think growth is the solution to economic crises and global warming?

RH: To support the dogma of growth is a heresy. I am the father of four boys. It would be terrifying if my children grew and grew, and just never stopped growing. It would be completely unnatural. Similarly, who would think to measure the success of their children by their size? Rather than growing endlessly, it's better that they reach their adult height, while gradually growing wiser, that they develop new skills, and expand their knowledge. In the same way, maintaining a model of unlimited growth in a limited world, is an aberration. Especially as this system puts all the power in the hands of a few. You can see this just by walking down the aisles of a supermarket: despite appearances, in recent decades our economy has been offering more and more products, but made by fewer and fewer multinationals. What is presented to us as a wider and freer selection of goods has actually reduced our options. For example, most of the beers we see on the shelves of supermarkets are, in fact, made by just five huge companies. Does that really represent choice really? The shelves have an ever-greater range of names, but the items are produced by an ever-smaller group of companies that enjoy a disproportionate amount of power. This concentration undermines social justice, democracy, and fairness.

Transition as job creator

LA: To prevent any real change, people who defend growth constantly say that ecology and restraint will lead to unemployment. What do you think? Does Transition have a positive impact on jobs?

RH: How can this argument still have any credibility at a time when the solar energy sector, for example, is creating far more jobs than oil or gas? The former is expanding rapidly, while the latter are undeniably in decline. Studies show that green energies and urban agriculture are a significant source of jobs.[1] The argument that we should improve growth to create jobs is false: when the economy is strong, it only benefits an elite few. In the last five years in the UK–since the economic crisis and the new Conservative government–the number of billionaires has doubled in the country, while 20% of employees only earn the minimum wage,

1. http://www.ilo.org/wcmsp5/groups/public/---ed_emp/---ifp_skills/documents/
publication/wcms_166823.pdf.

and basically live hand to mouth. The number of rich people has increased, as has the number of poor people. The inequality gap is widening. People with low incomes face housing costs that are far too high. It is simply inconceivable for anyone under the age of thirty to contemplate buying a house. One of the reasons that growth is inefficient is because of the insatiable appetite of investors and shareholders. They extract profit from regions far from where they're based, claiming it as their own. As I said, in my town of Totnes, maintaining and initiating local activities has created jobs, and multiple businesses serve the entire community: they organize and finance events in peoples' daily lives, they provide work to local suppliers, including support for our currency, etc. Why should the multinationals take away this wealth? Their goods all come from huge warehouses, and the few low-paid, precarious jobs they create by opening a store end up destroying many others.

Small is beautiful

LA: Is Transition creating jobs in other countries?

RH: Transition creates the conditions that encourage entrepreneurs to start their own businesses: for a caterer who wants to set up shop and source local products, the fact that a strong community is ready to offer support, and that local farmers are looking for outlets—and are ready to adapt to demand—is extremely motivating. I believe that the key development in the next five to ten years will be putting Transition at the heart of economic planning, because for the time being, most entrepreneurs remain highly traditional and often disconnected from the community.

LA: Your organization seems related to the Small is Beautiful philosophy: the initiatives are often organized by grassroots organizations (associations, local communities, small businesses). What about large companies? Do you have any example of major firms that are working with you?

RH: Yes, in Exeter. Not long ago, this town in southern England launched a local currency. Various types of businesses have moved there; among them, one of the largest is a Premier League rugby club, the Exeter Chiefs. It's one of the top teams in the country. It was created in 1871 and has a 10,000-seat stadium. The owner announced that he would accept the Exeter Pound at all their events, and also as currency for their business dealings, whether as printed notes or the cellphone-based payment version. Getting a business like this, one that is both powerful and strongly rooted in the community, is a brilliant idea. In addition to 1-, 5-, 10- and 20-pound Exeter bills, in 2015, when the town hosted the World Cup, it issued a limited 15-pound bill with the Exeter Chiefs on both sides of the note. Having a partner like this for Transition is also a way to expand an initiative to an entire swath of the community that would normally never get involved in a local currency.

Beyond this example, I must say that very few companies have tried out the principles of Transition. It's not because of their size, which is not an obstacle, but rather their lack of involvement in local economies. Major retailers like the Tesco supermarkets here in the UK are not interested in local economies. Yet they could have an extremely positive impact: both big and small companies purchase energy, food, services, and many other things. The way they source all this determines the role they play in the local economy. Large companies can also contribute by incubating the new economy: they can support those just starting out in a community by providing them with teams that could share skills and knowledge.

The local multiplier effect:
the crux of a worldwide movement

LA: What are the overall goals of these local projects? What is the founding principle of your vision for the economy?

RH: We want to help build an economy that will limit the climate increase to well below 2° Celsius over the preindustrial era of 1850 by 2100, ideally to bellow 1.5° Celsius. Today, major figures in the environmental movement, including Naomi Klein and Bill McKibben (founder of the NGO 350.org[1] which works to combat global warming) are saying that the real problem is no longer about finding new oil reserves, because we should stop burning it altogether; if we wait for the depletion of fossil fuels, it will be far too late. It is crucial to act now, so we should leave these fossil fuel sources untouched. This has led to the "Keep it in the ground"[2] and "Leave it in the ground"[3] campaigns. But this narrative raises several questions: If we leave it underground, what can we create above ground? What new model can we create? What kind of vision can we propose? Transition is providing answers to these questions. We can't just propose staying away from something, rejecting fossil fuels and growth. I much prefer the idea of moving toward a positive goal.

If our movement continues to grow as well as it has been, my feeling is that in twenty years' time, our companies and towns will have adopted a concept of economics that is much more embedded in a sense of place, and companies will be more strongly implanted locally. Our economy will be mostly based on the principle of the Local Multiplier Effect, developed by the New Economics Foundation

1. 350.org, http://www.350.org.
2. "Keep it in the Ground," *The Guardian*, http://www.theguardian.com/environment/series/keep-it-in-the-ground.
3. LINGO: Leave it in the Ground, http://leave-it-in-the-ground.org.

in London.[1] The idea is that when consumers spend 10 pounds in a supermarket or other chain store, it only produces 3.6 pounds of economic activity in their town. But if they shop in independent locally owned store, they generate activity of around 17.6 pounds, nearly five times as much. In short, if we want to create jobs at home, it's better to avoid opening large chain stores and instead opt for local businesses to maximum this multiplier effect.

Some initiatives, like the explosion of craft breweries around the world, demonstrate that this idea has already changed the way people think. Ten years ago, in America, just 1% of beer sold in the country was made in local breweries. The rest was Budweiser, Miller, and the other giants. Now 11% of beer is produced in independent craft breweries.[2] Many of these local, independent breweries are rooted in their communities. They are not centralized, but instead scattered all over the place, creating jobs that can't be delocalized. They don't have any goal of becoming market leaders, but are happy and proud to be sustainable, to use local raw materials, and to celebrate the culture of their communities. We are therefore looking at two different models. The first one concentrates wealth in the hands of a few. The second develops communities, creates jobs, and supports a new model: we are leaving behind a Budweiser culture for one that supports craft beer.

LA: What would you say to those who depend on this model of large centralized companies? To the men and women who work there or run them? Where does their future lie? Can they get involved in the development of Transition?

RH: It depends on the type of business they're interested in. For the person whose job involves importing plastic toilet seats made

1. New Economics Foundation, http://www.neweconomics.org.
2. "National Beer Sales and Production Data," Brewers Association, https://www. brewersassociation.org/statistics/national-beer-sales-production-data/.

in China, I would probably recommend changing their business model. Because this one–disconnected from the community and dependent on cheap, abundant oil–has no future. Some time ago I went to a meal with some bankers. We got to talking about local currencies. I told them about the various success stories, notably the Bristol Pound, and spread my local currency collection out on the table They reacted by saying: "That's amazing! They are very beautiful and cool! But doesn't it make life much more complicated for people?" I answered: "The point is, they make life more complicated for **you**, but actually for the rest of us, they can do things that the national currency can't." "Like what? Surely I can do everything with sterling, why do I need these?" "Because they work in a different way. Sterling does not bring communities closer together. Local currencies can do this; they build a different world."

Necessary changes to address shortages

LA: If you were the boss of a big company, it wouldn't be easy to totally overhaul your basic economic model. It would be like biting the hand that feeds you.

RH: I'd compare this to a company that has to change suppliers because of shortages. You want to be the first company to adapt, rather than the last. And the shift to a low-carbon economy is inevitable. Businesses can do it now, or in five to ten years. The ones who are preparing for it will be ahead of the curve, rather than having to react to it. They can surf on the wave, while others just may not make it. When CDs came in, all the factories pressing records cut their staff and started making CDs (although they are now making vinyl records again). When the Internet came in, all the people who worked in archiving paper files were put out of work. They had to change.

As things move forward, adjustments can be painful. But does this justify inertia? Should unemployment in the oil industry be a reason not to shift to a low-carbon economy? In a lower energy world, there will be winners and there will be losers, but far more winners in the long term: the economy will be more decentralized, more democratically owned, and the wealth will be distributed more fairly. I have met a lot of people working in the oil industry. When you talk to people off the record, people with children and families, they know the system they work for is reaching the end of the line. They're like everybody else, and share the same fears as others in their community. It's not surprising. And in fact, there are some very dynamic people who are pushing hard for change in their companies. When I was in the US, and met with the team at Transition Houston, the majority of them had backgrounds in the oil and gas sector, which I thought was fascinating.

In one oil company that does a lot of scenarios work, a few managers told me that among their projections, none of them include a future that would limit warming to under 2° Celsius. I asked them if they would be open to creating a scenario in which there are no oil companies: "Do you have a scenario that includes you not existing anymore?" They said yes, but they were probably only being polite. Shouldn't someone point out to them that the emperor doesn't have any clothes? When I meet somebody in an oil company, I always tell them that these companies need to be looking at themselves as tobacco companies see themselves: they are selling a harmful product. They can design a strategy by which the business contracts over time, in a gradual, realistic way, but one that remains profitable as it does so. Instead, these companies are still fighting efforts to create a low-carbon society, interfering with and hampering their progress, which is just criminal. There's a very strong possibility that in ten to fifteen years' time, they'll find themselves being prosecuted, just like drug dealers and criminals are today. The media recently reported that Shell is actively lobbying to undermine European Union renewable energy targets.[1] Some of the people running these companies are true psychopaths; they should probably not be holding these lofty positions of responsibility.

Multinationals survive only through our support

LA: The Transition movement has been expanding rapidly, but harmful multinationals like Monsanto don't consider them as any kind of substantial risk to their business model.

RH: Yes, there is the risk of expanding, but without having any influence on the system. That said, I saw Vandana Shiva speak in Dublin in 1996.[2] She said something that has stayed with me ever since: "These large companies and this system only exist because we give them our support. If we withdrew it, they couldn't function anymore." But to withdraw our support means that we need to have alternatives that we can pursue. One key way to fight giants like Monsanto and the others is to create a flourishing ecosystem of small- and medium-sized businesses that are reconnecting communities with the soil, the land around where they live, by retelling different stories, and creating different images around our food. To fight Monsanto, we not only have to keep seeds free and local, but also create businesses that sell the food

1. Arthur Neslen, "Shell Lobbied to Undermine EU Renewables Targets, Documents Reveal," *The Guardian*, April 27, 2015, https://www.theguardian.com/environment/2015/apr/27/shell-lobbied-to-undermine-eu-renewables-targets-documents-reveal.
2. Vandana Shiva is an Indian scientist and world-renowned environmentalist, known particularly for her support of free seeds.

they produce. If we cook delicious food with locally sourced products, everyone will want to be a part of it. Over the past fifteen to twenty years, we have seen a spectacular growth in interest in local food, in diversity, in taste.

We should build alternatives in such a way that they are more delicious, more nourishing, more enticing, and more fulfilling. Why would anybody want to work for Monsanto when they could work in a locally owned business, which has all kinds of beneficial impacts on the local community, in a business that people love? People want to do work that's loved, that they love. Why would you want to work for a multinational beer company when you could work in a craft brewery doing amazing things that people adore? The creation of many economically viable alternatives complements the work of people who are fighting back against the overreach of industrial giants. Transition takes a positive approach, but I have the deepest admiration for people who put their bodies on the line to say, "this far and no farther."

Involving friends and neighbors, adapting to a community's needs

LA: What if I wanted to create a small business in my community. How would you suggest I start? What key ideas should I follow?

RH: The common feature of new businesses is that they identify needs that aren't being met. For me, this process should include friends, neighbors, the local community; it should look at the area's needs from a broader perspective (economic, but also social), and see how a business can be part of a bigger picture, how it can meet wider needs. Building a membership from the beginning is very powerful. A couple in Yorkshire started a bakery called The

Handmade Bakery, based on a membership system with people who paid in advance for their bread every month. People were happy to support them, they felt like they had their very own bakers. When they wanted to expand and asked the bank for a loan, but it refused their request. So they went to their members and said: "Please invest in our business, we'll pay you 6% interest, but we will pay you that interest in bread." Everyone immediately invested! And as a business, it was capital that cost them around 2%. A membership network is therefore essential. This type of supportive model is very effective, and that's why the Local Entrepreneur Forum we organize is so powerful and exciting. This approach demonstrates the incredible force that's created when a local community gets behind its local businesses.

Intelligent short supply chains

LA: Can these multinationals you talk about continue to expand around the world, where infrastructure has been entirely designed and built to accommodate chain stores and long-distance trade? This situation has even challenged the effectiveness of short supply chains. In France, for example, the Commissariat Général au Développement Durable[1] studied the transport patterns of small producers who supply food to local markets. It saw that this short supply system was less efficient–per kilometers traveled–than cargo ships coming from far away. As opposed to trucks that go back empty, these boats are reloaded and never travel empty.

1. Rachida Boughriet, "Alimentation: le bilan carbone des circuits courts pointé par le CGDD," Actu Environmement.com, April 5, 2013, https://www.actu-environnement.com/ae/news/CGDD-bilan-carbone-circuits-courts-ademe-avis-socioeconomiques-18216.php4

RH: We have an infrastructure that favors supermarkets and centralized, long-distance trade: they have free parking, and the access
roads are often subsidized or even built by the government, because
they see shopping centers as a way of encouraging economic growth.
These big-box stores are extracting money out of local communities
and sending it to companies headquartered far away and to their
shareholders. We should look at systems like The Food Assembly[1]
and the Open Food Network,[2] to shift to relocalized food more
quickly. These sales networks connect local food producers with
consumers: people order on line from a wide selection of products
and pick up their produce at weekly pick-up markets organized by
The Food Assembly in the neighborhood where you live or work.
Short supply chains will only work if products become easy to buy,
with distribution methods that make buying local food easy, even
adopting certain things people like about supermarkets: the markets should be clean, bright, attractive, and accessible in terms of
technology–including a blog and Facebook page, complete with
recipe tips and information about the food producers. You order
online and can then meet the producers when you pick up your
food. Many people would be drawn to alternatives like this. There
is a fantastic CSA very near me. The women who run it make us
feel part of their adventure, part of the story of local producers.
We hear about when things go well, and when they don't. These
models make it more exciting to buy food, and tell a far better
story that the one told by supermarkets. Once these new distribution networks are well established, what will remain of large retailers? I'm not suggesting that the world would be a better place if
every supermarket closed tomorrow: many people feel that supermarkets are more practical from a logistics standpoint and remain
attached to this model. I sometimes have to go to a supermarket

1. The Food Assembly, https://thefoodassembly.com.
2. Open Food Network, https://openfoodnetwork.org/.

to buy certain products, because I can't afford to do all my shopping locally: there are six of us in the family, four of them hungry boys who eat a lot of food. I buy 50 to 60% of my food locally, something like that. I do shop in supermarkets, occasionally. But I pay attention to anything that I can buy locally. I much prefer shopping on the main street of my small town than in a shopping center: it's a nightmare dragging kids to a supermarket. They see all the colored packages of the industrialized food and try to get you to buy all kinds of stuff. In a good downtown shopping area, while I'm doing my errands, my kids can go off and meet their friends, play in the park, or help out by picking things up themselves, and meeting other people in the process. You don't get any of that in a supermarket.

LA: You mean to say that the logistical issues involved in short supply chains are part of a larger problem?

RH: Yes, if you look at it from a purely energy perspective alone, as in this CGDD report, you're missing the wider argument. These boats, for example, that bring food from hot climates, are indirectly extracting large quantities of water: the imported fruits, vegetables, and grain required massive irrigation to grow. We are therefore importing water from countries where it is desperately needed. Globalization has led to the loss of countless small farms, which have been gobbled up by agribusiness, both in the North and the South. That said, it would not be our intention to make England, Germany, and France entirely self-sufficient in terms of food. The idea is to aim for around 80% of locally produced food, as set out in the Growing Communities model discussed earlier. Trade between countries is beneficial. It has always existed, and indeed, is essential if we want to have certain products. Fife, a town in Scotland did a small-scale test aiming for 100% local food, called "The Fife Diet." But the people running the program quickly realized that when you ask people to eat only local food, the first thing they say is, "I can't live without chocolate, what about that?" They drew up a list of imported goods they felt they couldn't do without: red wine, of course, chocolate, bananas, tea, coffee, spices, and oranges. These were the main things; they represent about 20% of your diet. It's better not to try for a 100% local diet.

You need to factor in the economic aspect as well: spending a larger share of our money in local businesses is a very powerful booster, and everyone can do it. Even people with very low incomes who shop at supermarkets, thinking it's the cheapest option, will see that they can do at least 10% of their shopping locally, through cheaper local greengrocers. We don't have to go 100% local; if everyone managed a 10% shift, it would already have a significant impact. We could set up a kind of challenge, asking everyone to spend 5 pounds a week with local producers.

Younger generations: "We want to participate too!"

LA: Aside from your four sons, who have grown up in a world where Transition is omnipresent, how do you teach children, adolescents, and college kids about Transition. Are they interested?

RH: Young people are well aware of the problems that Transition deals with. The last time I went to Bologna, there was an event that brought together five high schools. About four hundred kids, aged fifteen to eighteen, participated. They specifically wanted to concentrate on food and on strategies for looking at food in different ways, through the framework of ecology. I was surprised to see how focused they were. One of the projects I discussed was run by two young men who started a business called GroCycle; it's an urban mushroom farm in Exeter. They have an unused office block where they grow mushrooms on old coffee grounds that they collect from bars and restaurants. I showed some pictures, and a group of students from each high school came up to me and said: "We want to do that, too!" Since then, the guys from Totnes GroCycle have traveled to Bologna to run a training workshop for these kids on how to start your own mushroom business. This means that when we present what we're doing in the right way, they pick up on it.

LA: Aside from these one-off initiatives, do you have any specific programs for young people?

RH: Over the years, we have done quite a lot of work with the secondary schools in Totnes. The first project was something called "Transition Tales":[1] we went into the schools and worked with them about what the world could be like in twenty years' time if we managed to inspire significant change by then. We then asked them to create a TV news program about everyday life in twenty years. They made up very funny stories; we filmed them and put them all on YouTube. We then expanded these initiative throughout the UK, to work with supporting schools that wanted to get involved in Transition. Ten to twelve schools around the country introduced a program called "Schools in Transition," and another one called "One Year in Transition," for eighteen to twenty-five year olds. In both programs, a group of young people get together and take on several projects in their own communities, then report back to their friends on their progress. It worked well. It's now starting in Portugal as well as in other countries. The University of St Andrews in Scotland has a very active Transition group that is working to improve the way the university operates, so that it makes better use of the land and is more resilient in a post-oil era. Other university

1. "Transition Tales," Youtube, 2:49, August 20, 2010, https://youtu.be/OG3uohj1myM.

initiatives include developing sourcing possibilities to provide locally grown produce to the campus restaurants and the students. They also run campaigns to raise awareness among students about our dependence on oil.

LA: What society will these young people inherit? How do you see the future of our economy? How will the situation evolve in the near future and in upcoming decades?

RH: A growing number of stakeholders in the finance sector are already refusing to invest in fossil fuels, and the ranks of those wondering how to overcome our dependency on oil is growing constantly. When we first began, people didn't understand, they used to look at me skeptically and ask: "Why are you spending so much energy on this?" But in hindsight, they now realize the relevance of this movement, and I no longer get this kind of reaction. In the meantime, we had acquired over a decade of experience.

Terry Leahy was head of Tesco for a long time. In an interview on the BBC, he once described small, local, independent economies as "medieval," including in this term everything that Transition is about. In fact, *his* argument is medieval. The idea that giving corporations and the 1% unfettered access to all your resources, to your markets, and to your people is starting to look quite dangerous and outdated. We will see power returned to the local level. During elections in the UK, one observer said, "Don't just vote." He was right; just voting is not enough, people need to get involved in all kinds of different ways. The economic regeneration that we are doing on a local scale will become mainstream in the next ten to fifteen years.

LA: You seem to be quite optimistic, even though our natural resources have never been under such a strain, or inequalities been so flagrant. Are the Transition initiatives able to tackle these challenges?

RH: Our seemingly unassuming approach contains a huge potential, which is constantly reaffirmed with the creation of large projects, as we have discussed, and with the many small-scale initiatives that are developing. I recently visited a Transition group in Berlin. They had planted thirty fruit trees in one of the downtown neighborhoods. It had been a lot of work to obtain permission, and the overall project had been difficult for those promoting it. It may have been somewhat discouraging to do all that just to plant a few trees. But the following year, the authority for that area of the city changed its policy, saying that everything they planted would henceforth be edible.

Putting in the effort to bring an idea to life, to make it concrete and visible, changes peoples' viewpoints and opens up new possibilities for those who watch it happen. Someone then just has to say, "Yes, of course!" and off they go. These developments always lead to a larger tipping point, even if no one can pinpoint exactly when and where it will happen. Many people's attitudes may already have been radically changed, even though we can't yet see the tangible results of this revolution.

3

RECONNECTING PEOPLE TO POLITICS, TO SOLIDARITY, TO THEMSELVES

A silent revolution,
beyond environmentalism

LA: The impact of Transition has now largely transcended the issue of peak oil. It launched the movement; is it still a priority?

RH: It hasn't been, for a few years now. We're talking more about the end of easy energy. That said, the peak oil analysis and its impact remain relevant: we've seen that the energy we're extracting now is ever-more expensive and has a larger carbon footprint. Furthermore, the very high price of oil was one of the key factors that triggered the global economic downturn in 2008. But arguments based on peak oil don't really resonate with people; they see cheap fuel at the pumps and read this nonsense in the newspapers that we're going to have fossil fuel around for years and years. For many consumers, the rest doesn't matter. Our message today is that if we wait until we've devoured all the fossil fuels, climate change will have become irreversible, and furthermore, that the solutions available to date (carbon offsetting mechanisms, biofuels) are not only ineffective, but are even counterproductive and dangerous. Even if we have never lived without oil–we were all born in the age of fossil fuels–it is indeed possible to live without it.

We had some terrible storms in Devon in February 2014. Our train line that connects us to the rest of the UK runs along the coast at a place called Dawlish, and in the storms the line collapsed into the sea, and meant we had no trains for several months while it was rebuilt. On the day of that storm I was riding my bike home and I got caught in the worst hailstorm of my life. I had to stop several times as the wind was blowing too hard and the intensity of the hail was really painful. When I finally got home, I felt quite traumatized. It's nothing compared to other regions that have experienced natural disasters linked to climate change. But this was the first time I had ever experienced anything so intense like that. The issue of climate change is huge. It's not just about putting solar panels on our roofs or driving more slowly; it's a much, much larger issue.

LA: How does your movement tackle this issue? How has it moved past the challenges of peak oil and global warming?

RH: Initially, Transition focused on practical solutions to these questions, but that's no longer the case today: in the meantime, entire segments of the society have realized that our economic model suffers from a more widespread, structural problem, even if people do not necessarily understand every cog in the system. They sense that our assessment is correct.

Peak oil was a starting point, and if we were to frame the reasons people are motivated to do Transition today, the list would be a long, and evolving one. I often discuss much broader topics during my talks. One of them is about the 1%, the wealthiest people who hold so much power. Opposing this, Transition is a quiet revolution of ordinary people around the world who are coming together to rethink and reimagine the places where they live. They are also addressing the harmful effects of a consumerist model, notably loneliness. They are innovating in the sectors of energy supply and finance. After nearly twelve years, I don't think we need to keep explaining what problem we are responding to. The profusion of amazing initiatives around the world is sufficient justification for Transition. This is the thing: creating a movement around a single issue means that you'll lose everyone who is not interested in that particular issue. Transition has always looked for ways to bring people together to deal with concerns that we can share with our neighbors, our friends, our community, and to work together. In short, beyond the formal issues that Transition is supposed to deal with, we encourage people to reinvent their lives, to achieve more resilience. That said, the energy issue is still at the heart of the movement.

Globalization is suffocating democracy, we are reviving it!

LA: How does relocalization promote democracy? The link between the two is not all that clear.

RH: Creating a resilient local economy gives communities a voice. Today, during election campaigns, if you listen to people's concerns, they're saying, "We need jobs! We need houses!" Candidates in the UK outdo each other talking about jobs and housing: "We will build more houses than you will! We will create more jobs than you will!" In their minds, any house is a good house, every job is a good job. I remember when Margaret Thatcher allowed Ronald Reagan to bring cruise missiles onto British soil. One of the reasons she gave that "It will create jobs," without making any distinction between what's a good job and what's a bad job. We now have a choice moving forward: we can create jobs that enrich the already fabulously wealthy 1%, or we can listen to local people and create other types of jobs that meet people's needs, that celebrate local culture and benefit the community.

The global economy–supermarkets are the perfect example–undermines the foundations of a community's democracy and its culture. When all the food you eat comes from a supermarket, you have imperceptibly internalized the fact that you have no power over the economy. In France and Italy, where food really matters, people are proud of their cuisine. When you stop in a small village for a meal, people tell you: "The recipe for this pasta that that we're serving today only exists here; you won't find it anywhere else. And the olive oil we make is absolutely the best in the world. The one they make in the village down the road, well, it's disgusting, you wouldn't even use it in a car engine." Unfortunately, supermarkets are killing this culture. Local initiatives, however, reconnect people with their communities and with local politics. They become as involved as these villagers who are so proud of their culinary heritage. In a book called, *How to Save Our Town Centres*,[1] urban planner Julian Dobson explains that we should create "places of possibility," a beautiful expression that really captures what Transition does.[2] It is about the kind of future we can create, the possibilities of reengaging people to make change happen.

Transition influences legislation

LA: Some Transition projects get bogged down by strict regulations. It's manageable when they remain small-scale, but what happens when they become larger. What obstacles, notably administrative, stand in your way?

RH: It's different in different places. When I meet people who are doing Transition in Italy, they tell me that for every project they want to do, there's a law against it. Even when they find the person who wrote the law and ask them why they added a clause blocking them, they honestly reply: "I don't know, I can't remember." There are places where it's very hard to accomplish anything. People in France and Belgium also face similar obstacles: every time a new idea comes up, people say they just hear about all the reasons why

1. Julian Dobson, *How to Save our Town Centres. A Radical Agenda for the Future of High Streets* (Bristol: Policy Press, 2015).
2. This idea is similar to that of the Pierre Rabhi's oases, places where tangible experimentation has inspired other initiatives.

they can't do them, especially when they involve energy initiatives. Here in the UK, however, this sector is one of the areas where interesting progress has been made: one of the big companies dominating the entire energy sector supports the principle of community cooperatives. Large companies in Germany have embraced and are supporting the idea. That's what I'd like to see develop further. Aside from these examples, in my experience, most obstacles to Transition exist only in our own minds.

LA: What do you mean? The many regulations that impact Transition do actually exist, don't they?

RH: Yes of course, but you can't let these obstacles stop you. Most often, the objections people come up with don't really exist. We don't realize our own potential, our power to simply act. To get past what is often a pointless reluctance, sometimes it's necessary to just keep moving forward and take action. There's a small town called Frome, in Somerset, UK, where people involved in Transition realized they needed more support from their local council. It was a very conservative council, so they formed "Independents for Frome," a completely apolitical group whose members agreed to work together, as independents, to achieve common goals. They were all voted into the council, which now supports Transition initiatives. They discovered that a town council actually has a wide range of powers, something that most people don't know: a council can borrow money, it can invest in property, buy buildings, issue shares, support local investment, and so on. Very few do these things because they don't know that they can. In Frome, they have since bought a building, started a farmer's market, invested in renewable energies, and created interesting housing projects. Rather than focusing on the things we fear and things we can't do, let's try to find the available methods that we don't know about and are not yet using. There are far more of them than you think.

LA: You flipped my question to focus on the unsuspected potential, rather than the obstacles.

RH: Yes, because this is very important to me: the old activist mindset tends to focus on all the things that are hindering change. We haven't exactly reached a situation with Transition where the police are kicking down your door and hauling you off to prison. This does happen in some places, and personally, I don't know if I'd have to courage to continue. But we have a lot more of freedom here. It's our job to claim it. Circling back to everything that can stop you is a way of staying comfortable. Some people say: "Community energy companies are great, but it will never happen in this town, because there are too many laws against it, no one will let us do it." There are not valid reasons: people should act, start projects; there will be plenty of time later to discover–or not–the obstacles to tackle. Other people have already done it, elsewhere, and in more difficult situations. It's just kind of lazy.

Here in the UK, we could have spent that last ten years saying: "When is the government going to tell us we can do community energy?" and remain hampered by all the obstacles standing in the way. But no, instead of complaining, we have done it! Communities all over the country have been starting their own energy companies. Some of these have been Transition; many others haven't. There is now a very good network of community energy projects across the country, along with a lot of peer-to-peer work. Some have raised large amounts of money from their own communities and even from institutions. Then, in 2014, Ed Davey, who was the government minister for energy and climate change, announced that he wanted a community renewables revolution. But it was already happening. When he wanted to launch this idea, he went to Brixton Energy, an initiative we discussed earlier, with solar panels on public buildings. He climbed up on the rooftop to have his photograph taken. Several months later, the government published a

Community Renewable Strategy. But Transition Network had helped to write it, and many of the studies it included were actually our case studies. The solution, therefore, is just do it! And then, sooner or later, the government tries to catch up with you. Governments are generally reactive, not proactive. Although subsequent to this, the government took a more fossil fuel-based approach and ditched some of the work, for me it still holds that this is a powerful way to influence government thinking. There's a huge amount you can accomplish just by launching a project. It starts to change the story, redefining the sense of what's possible and what's not. It develops a momentum.

LA: This experience in the energy sector demonstrates that Transition can impact governmental policy. Is this true in other areas?

RH: The Bristol Pound is another good example; there were already many others complementary currencies in existence, most of them quite small, in Totnes, Stroud, Lewes, Brixton, and in other countries. When the Bristol group wanted to introduce the currency to the entire city, they received a lot of media coverage. Once the news got out, the Bank of England called them to say: "Sorry? What are you doing? We think you need to come in and have a chat." The meeting lasted three hours. The Bank of English decided to allow the idea to go forward. In the end, to clarify the situation, it produced an official position paper on their understanding of local currencies, their legal status, how they work, and how they relate to the national currency. Once these currencies gained legitimacy, they started to sprout up everywhere, like mushrooms after the rain. This series of events illustrates how an idea that starts out small can grow large enough to even influence official tests.

The Atmos development in Totnes is another example, this time concerning urban planning. It proves that an existing law can even be used to support Transition. The Community Right to Build order we discussed earlier came about because of a recent law that gives local communities more control over local developments. If a group of people identifies a site and devises an overall plan that has involved community consultation, it can ask for a referendum. If 50% of voters approve the project, then planning permission is granted. This is therefore a new way to obtain a planning consent. This right already existed, but with Atmos, we are demonstrating how it can be used to regenerate the local economy. The project will primarily use local materials, produce more energy than it uses, create jobs, house local entrepreneurs, and be car free. In short, Atmos goes much farther than the legislators intended when they wrote this law. Some members of government now point to Atmos as an example of good practices to follow. It will therefore also improve the way elected officials support future projects.

The political impact
of an apolitical approach

LA: Transition's apolitical approach looks like a political tool.

RH: Yes, and yet many people say, "Transition is good, but it's not political enough." For me, it's the opposite; it is a profoundly political movement. What better way to demonstrate what we expect from governments? Is putting pressure on political authorities the best way to develop community energy companies? Should we demonstrate in the streets, demanding: "We want community energy companies now!" It might work. But we can also just start them up ourselves. The example in the UK, with the publication of the Community Renewable Strategy, which was inspired by our initiatives and those of other movements, shows that the government, which should have been in the forefront, ended up following the movement. It's better to start projects ourselves. If that isn't politics, what is?

Every town can have its own currency, its own energy company, its own construction company, and its own transportation and food systems. This shift is totally realistic, as tangible initiatives already exist in many communities, and we see that they can function in the long term. Transition Network links up all these projects. In the environment, the resilience of a natural milieu is the direct result of a dense system of interdependencies among all the species of plants and animals. We therefore want to weave together this new economy to create a vibrant, resilient ecosystem.

LA: It seems as if elected officials should be pursuing these Transition initiatives. How do they view them?

RH: In some towns and regions, elected officials are not interested in Transition. Others realize its importance and see that this approach can take on projects they can't do themselves, ones that can be extremely beneficial to the community. A council member in the town of Stroud, in the UK, told me: "If Transition Stroud didn't exist, we'd have to make it up." He could see the key role played by Transition in his town. In Bristol, the local currency wouldn't have happened if Transition Bristol hadn't spent three or four years building up a good relationship with the city council. They had established mutual trust and respect, so that when they brought up the idea for the Bristol Pound, the council was excited and enthusiastic about making it happen. The Exeter Pound came about because the head of the council was really impressed by the experience in Bristol. They realized that the council and Transition needed to support each other to make it happen. I think that any kind of enlightened local politician will recognize that Transition is not a threat, but rather an enormous opportunity. The movement can take risks in a way that local governments struggle to do, especially during times of imposed austerity.

LA: What would you advise politicians you meet? Would you tell them to leave their mandate and participate in the Transition movement, because the political system itself blocks important changes, or rather stay inside the political system to change it from within?

RH: The political system exists, and we need good people in it, people who understand the problems, who understand the possibilities, who act with integrity. Politicians are therefore useful and necessary. But to me it appears that the higher people rise in any organization (whether in business or politics), the less creative, imaginative, and more risk-averse they become. Most of the exciting, innovative, creative things in a society are happening at the grassroots level. If some of these people carry their convictions to higher levels of politics, they can really start to make changes–although I can only imagine the stress and exhaustion of implementing ideas like Transition at that point.

I would say that the role of each level of government is to reflect and implement the ideas and needs of individuals. It's therefore very important that these people remain connected to what's happening on the ground, that they continually ask: "How can I help?" We need politicians who can be outspoken and straightforward, which is not the case today; otherwise they wouldn't be talking about maintaining growth, but rather how we can survive in an endangered biosphere. This situation is creating the most extraordinary opportunity for both decision-makers and ordinary people to be brilliant, bold, and imaginative.

LA: You say that the higher people rise in political or economic levels, the fewer risks they take, the less creative they are. Transition, however, is built on these ideas.

RH: Yes, absolutely. Transition doesn't have anything to lose, there is no power or money at stake. Transition groups can therefore be nimble, fast, responsive, playful, and creative in ways that bigger organizations can't.

When we started Transition Network, the foundation that initially funded us (The Tudor Trust) gave us a first bit of advice: "Do not become a membership organization. Do not become one of those NGOs that spends all its time and energy keeping its membership happy, producing newsletters, and so on. What we love about Transition is that you're fast, you're quick, you can just do things. Stay nimble!" What I see is that the larger an organization gets, the more inertia there is, the harder it is to act. Transition has to stay light on its feet: if we get to the stage where we employ two hundred people, it means that something has gone horribly wrong. Our idea is always to give away whatever power we have, whenever we can.

Transition combats austerity measures in countries hit by crises

LA: The wealthiest elements of society have the power to block improvements in living standards for the rest of society. The crisis in Greece is a good example. Does the movement have any influence over this?

RH: New Transition groups are constantly being formed in southern Europe, in Greece, Spain, and Portugal. There are lots of groups in Spain; in fact, the first non-English book about Transition was put out by an independent publisher in that country.[1] It's a Transition

---

1. Juan del Río, *Guía del movimiento de transición. Cómo transformar tu vida en la ciudad,* introduction by Rob Hopkins (Madrid: Libros de la Catarata, 2015).

guide. Lots of people in these countries have adopted Transition as a response to austerity, as a way to reclaim local control. In Portugal, one of the first Transition groups, in Portalegre, soon realized that it had to work in quite a different way than how we do things in northern Europe. They're pursuing Transition in a place where people have no money. If you show a film and you charge four euros to come and see a video, people won't come, because they need those four euros. Transition there functions around the idea of a gift economy and generosity. In Transition, we have a term we call "the power to convene." The way it works, is they ask the community what they would like to do and then help them accomplish it. When, for example, a community says: "We'd like a shared garden for our building," they mobilize forty people who come and work. No money changes hands, but projects get done.

Shortly after the stock market crash that triggered the crisis, the mayor of Portalegre, who had always been dismissive of Transition, finally came to the group and asked for their help: "The council doesn't have any money, and I don't know what to do." They developed a way of working with the town council; they even ran a festival all around the idea of the gift economy. The town didn't have any money, but it supports them in lots of other ways: it lets them use the printing press in the mayor's office, gives them venue spaces, and so on. Transition therefore looks very different, depending on the local context. In Belgium, a Transition group can raise 1,850,000 euros to fund a vineyard, but that wouldn't happen in Portugal or Greece. But even if there is very little money, Transition still has a very powerful role to play in terms of reinventing the economy, bringing people together around a project, and maintaining communities dealing with stress and poverty.

No replacement for public services

LA: Can Transition help people break out of the poverty trap, those who depend on social help, the poor, and those who are over-indebted? Social tensions continue to grow. What is Transition's response?

RH: We need to be careful about this: the government has introduced austerity measures and is constantly cutting public services, but it cannot depend on us to take over these responsibilities. In Totnes, for example, many of the services once provided by the council have been handed over to private companies to run. There is a real tension here between stepping up to take opportunities on behalf of the community, seizing the opportunities that are emerging, and avoiding any action that would collude in the unraveling of the social contract. In the wake of Hurricane Sandy, Noam Chomsky wrote about what he called "Occupy Sandy": a lot of the Occupy Wall Street groups became first responders to people who were hit by the hurricane. They often arrived sooner than the FEMA people did. He concluded: "The trouble is, it is a double-edged sword, because to the extent that Sandy or other citizens efforts are effective, they reduce the pressure on the federal government to stand up and do what it is supposed to do. That is a trap you want to be able to avoid. ... The trouble with saying 'the government backs off' is that it only feeds the libertarians. The wealthy and the corporate sector are delighted to have government back off, because then they get more power. Suppose you were to develop a voluntary system, a community type, a mutual support system that takes care of social security—the wealthy sectors would be delighted."[1]

1. Jeff Smith, "Chomsky on Mutual Aid, Occupy Sandy and Unions in Michigan," GRIID, February 27, 2013, https://griid.org/2013/02/27/chomsky-on-mutual-aid-occupy-sandy-and-unions-in-michigan/.

Here, in a country where the government is constantly cutting back public services, I'm not sure I agree with Chomsky. It is part of our role to step in and offer alternatives, as we can do a far better job than the Sodexos of this world. The Evergreen Coops in Cleveland, Ohio, have been a real inspiration to us in this regard.

LA: Can populations at risk get involved with Transition when they are struggling to just get by?

RH: I don't think it's realistic to expect a single mother who's living on very little money, who's working to try and support a family, to have time to get involved in Transition. The reality is that now, Transition works with people who have the time, financial security, and skills to contribute to our movement. It's somewhat inevitable at this stage. But at the same time, Transition has a duty to remain open and inviting, inclusive of all people–if only to bring together people from different backgrounds to offer an alternative to solitude and isolation by creating events. Transition can also foster the creation of new enterprises for and by residents, based in the community, thereby creating jobs.

This question of poverty brings up an important point, which is that Transition doesn't do everything. Many of the criticisms we get revolve around this: "How is Transition going to overturn neoliberal capitalism?" some people ask. Or: "How is Transition going to help the world go vegan?" Unfortunately, the movement cannot respond to all these questions. It's more like an app on your phone, designed to do one thing, very skillfully. It is social technology that helps you, in a methodical way, make the place where you live more resilient, to bring people together, where they feel part of a movement that is reinventing the future. When people ask, "What is Transition doing in the search for a cancer cure?" my answer is "Nothing."

Less technology, more social innovation

LA: Transition is more a social innovation than a technological innovation. Where does technology fit into your vision? You've said that Transition would never have been this successful without the Internet.

RH: Many people believe the dangerous illusion that technology can do everything. I did a TED talk in 2008. These events offer a forum for ideas that deserved to be shared to the largest possible audience. Even though many of these short presentations are fascinating, the TED culture tends to be a bit self-satisfied: "We are so brilliant that we can innovate and invent our way out of problems." It's all about gadgets, computer programs, and technology. These innovations obviously have a role to play, but I don't buy into the idea that we can merely turn on a 3D printer to stamp out a sustainable future.

LA: Do you think technology has already spread far enough in our society and that we already have the necessary tools to save the planet without looking for new ones? How can Transition contribute at this level? How can it change our relationship to technology?

RH: People are always inventing new tools, it's what we do. But we should also make social technologies more attractive. I hear the term "smart cities" quite a lot; they are primarily based on new technologies. But do they encourage people to have more conversations with each other? If everything is "smart," then why do we need to talk to each other? Does technology replace people sitting on a bench like this and having a conversation, because we don't need to anymore?

The invasion of technology in our lives pushes us to own multiple machines and tablets, but these devices should instead be designed for purpose rather than possession. We should keep in mind that they perform services; we don't necessarily need to actually own all these things. Take telephones, for example: I don't need a phone per se; what I need is the ability to contact people. The same goes for washing machines: I don't need to own the machine, I need to be able to clean my clothes.

Encouraging a service economy that is more circular and collaborative can parallel technological growth. Unfortunately, circular economies are increasingly the domain of big businesses, which share and become more efficient. From an ecological point of view, it's useful. But from a power and economics perspective, it just makes the neoliberal, capitalist system that much more efficient, without benefiting local economies, the society at large, and democracy. A circular economy is one in which resources are not just extracted, used, then thrown away, according to a traditional linear trajectory, but instead are extracted and then recycled and reused constantly. Transition is not about this kind of single circle, but a multitude of circular local economies. The real question is this: How to implement and optimize this kind of system? It's not about technology. Technology can certainly help circular local economies, but it's no replacement for them. Smart cities aren't enough; we need convivial cities, conversational cities. We need cities that roll their sleeves up. If we want a major city to grow 5% of its food within the city, technology has a role to play—how do you put rooftop gardens atop buildings, how do you manage the water—but what matters is how you make people want to do this. How do you communicate it? How do you tell a story about it and what's the design? All these things are as important as the technology.

Relearning manual skills

LA: In addition to its basic themes, Transition also encourages people to work with their hands and relearn practical skills, including a closer connection to the earth.

RH: Yes, Transition encourages everyone to learn skills. In fact, we have a specific "skill-share" program. People come who have skills to offer, for free. They teach people how to work with wood, grow plants, and so on. This kind of transmission is very valuable, because once we start to lose these skills, it's very hard to get them back again.

When I was eighteen and had just finished my exams, I went to school to get the results—which weren't impressive at all—and I remember sitting outside in the morning sunshine, on the last day I would ever be at that school. I was with all my close friends and I remember thinking, "We are so useless." Between us, we could hardly have done anything manual. If we were all washed up on a desert island, we wouldn't even know how to eat each other! As people, as communities, it's important and powerful to become more skilled.

I recently met a woman named Sarah Corbett,[1] who does something called "craftivism," a kind of activism through craft. She teaches people to make small hand-sewn things that carry statements and messages. In the UK, a study commissioned by the insurance company Lloyds TSB revealed that over the last ten years, the average attention span has fallen from twelve to five minutes because of social media, computers, and television.[2] Her idea is that working with your hands is a very powerful way to rebuild that attention and

1. Rob Hopkins, "Sara Corbett: Changing the World One Backstitch at a Time," Transition Network.org, March 9, 2015, https://transitionnetwork.org/news-and-blog/sarah-corbett-changing-the-world-one-backstitch-at-a-time/.
2. Matthew Moor, "Stress of Modern Life Cuts Attention Spans to Five Minutes," *The Telegraph*, November 26, 2008, http://www.telegraph.co.uk/news/health/news/3522781/Stress-of-modern-life-cutsattention-spans-to-five-minutes.html

concentration span. Another Transition member who coordinates the various national Transition hubs used to work in the European Parliament, and still sometimes represents the Transition Network in Brussels. She knits a great deal; she says that knitting during meetings slows down her mind enough so that she can concentrate on the proceedings.

Inner Transition: in support of collective mindfulness

LA: When Transition first developed in Totnes, you placed a great deal of importance on the psychological health of those working with the movement, through the Inner Transition program. Given the many people involved around the world, can this approach still be applied within groups to maintain harmonious working relationships?

RH: The program is one of our priorities, because unfortunately, many of the groups I meet with have not yet integrated Inner Transition, a process that involves organizing meetings to deal with the way the group operates and to foster understanding among members. Their meetings are all about the work they have to do. They don't have any way to manage conflict, so they work hard to keep a lid on any conflict. It's the elephant in the room. I've been part of movements in the past that ended up being suffocated by the weight of the elephants in the room. It's important that Transition be an organization that can befriend its elephants, take them for a walk in the park rather than be squashed by them. Over the next few years, I think we should prioritize the tools of Inner Transition to make groups more resilient. The people who get involved in this movement don't come because it's this year's trend. For many of them, it becomes their life's work, a full-time occupation. People should then love it; it should make them stronger. There's no future for us if it becomes a burden and people say, "No, not another meeting!" We are now raising awareness among our members about the methods of Inner Transition so that, as in Totnes, they can benefit from it as much as possible.

LA: An elephant is quite large; how do you get it out of the room? What are these meetings like?

RH: Transition can be a difficult burden for a group to carry: it combines inner work to change our own habits and behaviors, with the outer aspect of practical initiatives. These two elements form a whole. Our program aims to provide individuals with more resilience. These are the key strands of the meetings. There are many ways to go about it: some groups read books or watch a film, followed by a discussion. Others organize activities meant to reconnect with nature, in an environment conducive to examining these issues. And finally, as I have already discussed, everyone who works at the heart of the movement has free psychological support available at any time they want, provided by professionals. When we ask groups who use Inner Transition how they feel about this work, they say their relationships with others are stronger and they feel recharged, with the necessary energy and confidence to move forward. This practice also fosters more compassion, detachment and clarity toward any particular situation that must be dealt with. Many people who started using the program from the beginning had already been practicing yoga or meditation. They compare Inner Transition to a form of collective mindfulness. Members develop a combination of detachment and attentiveness that improves the overall ambiance. These meetings are places where everyone can open up and share their doubts and vulnerabilities, as a way of developing trust, compassion, and tolerance within the group.

LA: Transition draws some of its principles from psychology, but also from other disciplines, including philosophy, politics, and practical ecology. What books have most inspired you?

RH: My thinking has been shaped by books on emancipation movements, music, and obviously, agriculture. I am especially drawn to people who write about practical ecology: the great permaculture experts like David Holmgren and Bill Mollison,[1] two Australians who developed the concept and methods of permaculture, as well as others who specialize in straw-bale construction, like Barbara Jones,[2] who was influential in spreading knowledge about this technique. I have also been inspired by System theory authors, including the American physicist Fritjof Capra, who advocates abandoning the scientific rationalism that promotes specialization and compartmentalization. He supports a more holistic vision, based on the interdependency of elements that are erroneously viewed as distinct, simply because we haven't taken the time to study the relationships that connect them. Otherwise, I am greatly inspired by the stories and scenes in books by Charles Dickens, notably *Great Expectations*,[3] which I think is one of the greatest works ever written. There's a scene about a guy who has a farm in the middle of London, where he raises his own fish. I would also recommend American ecologist Aldo Leopold, who wrote one of the seminal works on deep ecology, *A Sand County Almanac*,[4] which supports the principle that the earth itself has inalienable rights.

Other iconic figures, not necessarily linked to environmental issues, have also been important to me: Rosa Parks, for example, the black woman who refused to give up her seat on a bus

1. David Holmgren and Bill Mollison, *Permaculture One* and *Permaculture 2*.
2. Barbara Jones, *Building with Straw Bales: A Practical Manual for Self-Builders and Architects* (Cambridge: Green Book, 2015 [3rd edition]).
3. Charles Dickens, *Great Expectations* (London: Penguin Classics, [1861] 2002).
4. Aldo Leopold, *A Sand County Almanac* (New York: Oxford University Press, 1949).

to a white person in the segregated South. But I also draw from the punk and post-punk period, when we were listening to a lot of independent music. These people, including Tom Vague and Matt Haynes, were writing, publishing and selling their own, highly compelling fanzines. One of them was called *Are You Scared to Get Happy?*, and another one, by Tom Vague, adopted the layout of *Vogue*, but he titled it *Vague* instead. I loved the freedom and passion they expressed. Transition was widely inspired by their vision, which motivates us to pursue our ideas, and above all, to create the future we want, without waiting for permission or for anyone else to do it for us.

No guarantees, nothing in return

LA: Transition has always been very inclusive. You yourself are always trying to step back and push others forward. In a society where pride and narcissism are often seen as qualities, this behavior many seem surprising. What's the philosophy behind this?

RH: I have always been inspired by the Buddhist idea of the bodhisattva,[1] which refers to someone who lives their life in the service of others. I have tried to bring this idea of humility into the workings of Transition. It's a compassionate process, a service. It's not about huge egos and building empires. This is how we set things up, where no one person holds too much power. With this approach, we often encourage Transition groups to start with an "initiating group," designed from the outset for its own demise; it is not meant to remain through to the final project. This steering group comes together to launch Transition in a community. Once

1. See note p. 29.

the foundations have been created, they transmit all this to others, and they can, of course, continue to serve in a different capacity.

I've been to a couple of events where people worked very hard to start a Transition group: they gave a year of their time, they ran awareness-raising campaigns, created a website, opened a bank account. They essentially created the structure. Then once they were done, they held a big event and said: "We're stepping back now. If this is to continue, other people have to take on the project." I love this process: when you've created something you love, it's very hard to give it away. It's like putting your child up for adoption. It can be terrifying.

People sometimes notice this kind of humility in Transition, and that's important to me. It's about being mindful of what's called the "founder's syndrome"–whereby people start companies, a political party, or an NGO, and then stay on for too long. They end up being obstacles within the organization they themselves created. For me, I was deeply involved in Transition Town Totnes for about four years. After that, I deliberately took myself out of the steering group and the core group. I'm still active in some of the projects, but I'm no longer at the center of the process. I think it's better all-around for the group. You can't cling to it, just because you came up with an idea. It makes some people a bit crazy, thinking that they'll lose all control of what they founded. They say: "My God, without me, they'll all lose their way!" No, you just have to let go of all that.

LA: Was it hard for you to step down?

RH: Yes, it was quite hard in the beginning, but not as bad as all that. Do you remember the story I told you about the executive? He was joking about that fact that we had created an amazing brand and given it away to Transition groups for free? I told him that the essential difference between my world and his is that there is a lot of trust in this one. Transition works because of trust. We don't try to control the movement, and haven't seen any questionable behavior. We haven't yet had a Transition group started up by neo-Nazis or had any financial scandals. None of that has happened because there is a huge amount of trust. Transition says: "Here's a highly effective tool; take it, do something remarkable with it, we trust you to do this." It's exciting and refreshing to work within a movement that doesn't claim to have all the answers. We like to be able to admit that we don't know the answer to certain questions. This spirit has been with the movement from the start.

LA: You seem to let your organization take its own natural path, like a gardener who organizes a vegetable plot or orchard according to the behavior of certain plants, including wild plants. Have you been inspired by deep ecology?

RH: Yes, certainly. I love Joanna Macy's work on deep ecology. This Californian author wrote an incredible story, based on true events, that's included in her book of short stories and essays, *World as Lover, World as Self.* It's about a Tibetan lama who returns to Tibet after the Chinese occupation, with the idea of rebuilding his monastery. The monks work every day without knowing if their structure will still be standing the following day. Despite the constant uncertainty–a metaphor for the environmental crisis–they trust their deeper nature and instinct for survival. This woman, a great Tibetan Buddhist scholar, actually went and spent time working with this monk to rebuild the monastery. Joanna Macy's work has inspired many people in Transition.

LA: How does the story end? What message is Joanna Macy trying to convey, notably on the theme of deep ecology?

RH: The lama who threw himself into this project managed to bring other monks back to work with him. Those with more experience taught the younger ones, creating a positive dynamic as they built. The villagers were also drawn into the energy of the project and joined in. Finally, this monastery meant everything to them. By the end of the story, Joanna Macy draws a wider analogy: we are all like this monk, working to make the world a better place, even though we have no idea if it's going to work.

We are imitating the plant and animal worlds, which continuously regenerate without any concept of the future. There's no guarantee, whether you're involved in Transition or in something else. Everything can change tomorrow. Yet despite this uncertainty, you keep building the future, brick by brick. Simply because it's the right thing to do, without expecting to get any credit for this work.

That said, there are areas of deep ecology I'm not so sure about. I think it's an exaggeration and somewhat naïve when deep ecology purports to say nature does everything better than people, that the closer you are to nature to better you are, that cultures and civilizations most closely linked to nature are purer and more advanced. There are many horrible things in nature, and I think it's probably a good thing that we've devoted a time and money to keep it a bay at times.

LA: The reality is far from Joanna Macy's optimism. Other people, like Naomi Klein, for example, say that climate change will trigger authoritarian reactions from governments and a sort of eco-fascism. What do you say?

RH: What we're seeing now is quite the opposite: we see many people arguing that climate change isn't even a problem, so we don't yet need to be concerned about overzealous ecologists. Worrying, like Naomi Klein, about what will happen when we get to three or four degrees warming is a way to make yourself extremely miserable. I still think there is a small, but real possibility that we can take things in hand and alter the scenario. I'd rather give all my energy trying to make that happen rather than speculating about what might happen when we reach that extreme. Because by the time we hit three or four degrees, we'll probably have lost the game. Yes, maybe there will be eco-fascism or a new religious cult, who knows? But it's too early to worry about it. I read Naomi Klein's book, *This Changes Everything*,[1] and I must say that it was frustrating, because I had to read through 350 pages before she mentions the idea of modeling solutions at a local level.

But I think she's fantastic, and I especially like the line where she says: "There are no non-radical solutions left." Some people may be terrified by this statement because they have a negative idea of this word "radical." But it can also be something extremely positive, hopeful. From a Transition perspective, we read Naomi Klein's analysis and say: "Fantastic! Brilliant! Let's do it!" This outlook sets aside sham solutions that say throwing up a few solar panels on a rooftop would make everything fine. No. We need to rethink scale, we need to rethink our system, and be bold and creative. The next revolution will not be an industrial one, but rather cultural– even though the term "cultural revolution" has too many unfortunate connotations to be acceptable! We are extraordinarily lucky; it's a wonderful time to be alive. If you're twenty years old now, you could be looking at the start of an amazing change.

A positive scenario

LA: How is Transition preparing for the next few years. Do you have any major projects in the works?

---

1. Naomi Klein, *This Changes Everything: Capitalism vs. the Climate* (New York: Simon & Schuster, 2014).

RH: First of all, our mission is not just to spread the idea of Transition everywhere. We also do long-term support and follow-up work, through which we can assess our progress. To better structure and improve this process, we are now devising indicators to be used in an organizational tool. We are creating this with the help of researchers from University of Oxford and the Low Carbon Communities network, which connects many local groups working to combat climate change.

We also have a project to improve our communications, to better explain the Transition approach, and also to make it more visible; this is essential. The Brixton group had an inspired idea: their 10-pound note has David Bowie on it. Every movement needs its icons, its banners, and this offbeat idea gave them all kinds of publicity. I saw it when I went to Paris recently, at an event in Pré-Saint-Gervais, which has a Transition group. There were a lot a people gathered around their urban garden when the mayor came along. He wanted to have his photograph taken, not with me, not with the local Transition group, but with the David Bowie 10-pound note! I have taken that note to talks all around the world, and every time I hold it up, it gets a round of applause before I even say anything. This simple, but funny note is very powerful. It is both a beautiful piece of design and a great story. We need more symbols like this, which can tell the story of Transition in different ways. It's very important and is one of our upcoming projects.

LA: There's a gap between your easygoing personality and the serious questions you address. Is it really optimism or just a posture to motivate the movement?

RH: Whenever I get asked a question about optimism, I repeat something Paul Hawken said during a graduation speech: "If you look at the science about what is happening on earth and aren't pessimistic, you don't understand data. But if you meet the people who are working to restore this earth and you aren't optimistic, they you haven't got a pulse."[1] This really resonates with me. I try not to get stuck on whether I'm an optimist or a pessimist. We are often a bit of both. Optimism in the face of everything seems shallow to me, but in general, I am filled with hope about the human spirit and our ability to do remarkable things, and the considerable impact that can be achieved by a relatively small number of people working with integrity, compassion, humility, and purpose.

History offers many remarkable examples of successful resistance movements and struggles. But creating a positive scenario also requires people who can weave a compelling narrative of the future. Its potential seems obvious: while keep beating your head against a wall when there's a positive, realistic, and fun alternative? This is one of the basic principles of nonviolence. The Civil Rights movement did this beautifully, with "I have a dream." Alongside the people who are building a new future are others who refuse the current situation; these are two complementary approaches. It's crucial to say no and oppose harmful projects like new coal mines and fracking. But at the same time, we need a positive vision that's not just nebulous, but one that people can already see, touch, and smell. A vision that doesn't require you to agree to a whole list of things before you can even join.

A quiet revolution is happening today in towns, cities, villages, neighborhoods, and even institutions, where remarkable people are making things happen. English author David Nobbs recently wrote a humorous novel called *The Second Life of Sally Mottram*. It's the story of a woman who starts her own Transition group. I thought it was fascinating. This story shows that Transition has become mainstream enough to be part of everyone's culture. David Nobbs is not an activist, he's not a radical, he's not associated with the

1. An American entrepreneur, ecologist, and author on books about sustainable development. "You are Brilliant, and the Earth is Hiring," commencement address to the Class of 2009, University of Portland, May 3, 2009.

issue of climate change, yet he wrote a very funny and moving novel about a woman whose town was dying, where the shops were closing, the young people moving away. She visits Totnes and says, "I could do that!" and then goes home and tries it. For me, it's not so much about optimism; it's a belief in human beings' ability to do remarkable things.

The word I most hate to see associated with Transition, however, is "utopian"–when people say that's what we're working toward. No, it's not at all about that. Because a utopia is something that's never going to happen. When I imagine a society with local food, agroforestry, buildings constructed from local materials, and renewable energy, that's no utopia. It's a viable mix of several things that already exist in my world. It brings together my friend Dave's garden, the amazing straw-bale and clay plastered house of another friend, a renewable energy company I know of. It's not a fantasy at all. This is basically about taking intelligent and realistic alternatives from here, others from there, and putting them together to form a new society, and then scaling up the solutions. We only talk about tangible proposals, based on conclusive and practical experience. Obviously when people come to visit Totnes, they don't see a perfect city. Some of them leave disappointed, because they thought they would see some kind of eco-Shangri-La, with wind turbines everywhere and houses made of bales of straw with goats grazing on all the rooftops. About 90% of what Transition does is under the surface. Even so, most people quickly understand this after meeting the townspeople, and they take home a realistic view of what's happening. Since we began this movement, we have become aware that it is very much a cultural process.

LA: How effective is this invisible process. How does it work?

RH: People involved in a movement are used to very linear processes: they run a campaign hoping that people will hear their message and follow it. They then measure the impact of their awareness-raising work to assess whether they've been successful or not. Transition doesn't work anything like that. It's more like a mycorrhizal fungus, a very fine fungus that runs under the surface; it's so small that you can hardly see it. It forms an inextricable network that produces a rich humus, feeds a forest, and gives a woodland its resilience. It distributes nutrients and ensures the balance of the ecosystem. It's almost like the brain of a forest. Taking this as our metaphor, in 2006, we inoculated Totnes with a Transition mycorrhizal culture, and it runs under the surface. Sometimes it fruits in places where you expect it; and sometimes in far less predictable places. It doesn't matter: Transition lets it run wherever it wants to go. If you're a control freak, Transition is not for you. It involves a lot of trust, a lot of confidence that the right people will pick it up. This kind of operating mode often generates serendipitous situations. For example, just when we're looking for someone who knows how to do one thing or another, we're often surprised to discover that they were nearby all along. The right people and the right skills usually show up at the right moment, due in large part to this trust and flexibility. If you try to run something too rigidly, this type of thing doesn't happen.

An extraordinary opportunity

LA: You talked about your Inner Transition program as an antidote to burn-out. We have just spent a few days together and you don't seem stressed at all. Before we end, can you tell us how you organize your own life to avoid overwork?

RH: The first thing is that the Transition Network isn't just me. We have a team of about a dozen or so people, and they're all fantastic.

For me, I learned a lot from my experience working on my degree. When I was twenty-four, I went back to university for a degree in Environmental Quality and Resource Management, one of the first sustainability degrees available in Bristol. I started taking classes when my son was three months old, and my second son was born a few weeks before my final exams. For lots of people going to university, life was relaxed: they'd go to lectures, head to the café, sit on the grass. For me, it was like a job. I couldn't study once I got home and couldn't stay up all night either. My work slot was tight: I got to university at 9:00 a.m., left at 5:00 p.m., and squeezed in every minute I could to study efficiently. I developed a very focused and disciplined work culture that I still maintain. I try hard to be home by 5:30 p.m.; every day, it's very important to me. At night, I only work after my kids are in bed and if my wife is also working. I try to never work on weekends. It doesn't always work, but I try very hard to do that. To maintain this pace, I wake up quite early, around 6 a.m., and normally do one and a half to two hours of work before my children get up.

I was once invited to a party for the chief executive leaving a major UK environmental NGO. I asked him: "What's going to really change in your life?" He said: "Not working seven days a week." He had worked seven days a week, as his children grew up without him; I thought that was tragic. I think it's important that we model the kind of culture we want to create. That's the reason I gave up flying in 2006, and that's why I'm a vegetarian. I have despaired of all those international experts on climate change who spend all their lives in airplanes. We've created Transition Network in forty-seven countries, and I have only taken an airplane once in the last ten years (I went to the US in 2013). This is crucial for me. We use Skype and video conferencing to stay in touch with Transition groups around the world, and that's usually sufficient. Adopting this lifestyle also means growing my own food; the garden is not huge, but we produce a lot of food in a small, intensively farmed space, and we have a few chickens running around. I had to put some kinds of firebreaks in place when we moved to Totnes, to protect my family time, to set limits so that my involvement didn't affect our lives.

LA: Why this decision at that time?

RH: My wife and I had a traumatic experience in Ireland that pushed us toward a better balance, where family life and professional life are kept separate. When we lived in Ireland, we started working to create one of the first ecovillages. After obtaining planning permission, which was very difficult to get, we started to build two houses: one for us, the other for a training center. These were the first new cob-buildings constructed in Ireland in over one hundred years. Hundreds of volunteers came to learn on the site and help us put the buildings up. This represented a culmination, both on a professional and personal level, of all that we'd been committed to. When it was nearly finished, there was a fire, set deliberately, that burned our house down. We didn't have any insurance. After doing everything we could to put out the fire, we just sat on the grass and watched our house burn. It was deeply traumatic. But what was most remarkable was that some friends put together an amazing "Not in my name" campaign. They organized fund-raising efforts, with concerts, events, pub quizzes, anything that would raise money. In the end they raised 40,000 euros, and let us know that they didn't expect us to reinvest in rebuilding there, given how difficult it had been for us. They wanted to compensate us for the money we'd lost, but with no expectation as to what we'd do with it. This fire did not only destroy the houses, it also left our life project in ashes. We had wanted to live and work there with our family. We loved this house that we had literally built with our own hands. If we hadn't had that fire, we'd still be living there. Since then, I have been very careful about separating family time from my work with

Transition; before, it was all mixed together, and the fire affected it all. This decision is the best way for me to protect my family life.

But this experience is also a story about providence. If we had stayed there, in that fairly isolated place, Transition as we know it know and its development around the world would probably never have happened. It's funny how life works out. It was the right thing, but the wrong place; life therefore took us somewhere else, to Totnes and to Transition, which this time, flowed so much better. This town is the best place we could have found for this project. In a way, moving to Totnes turned out to be the greatest thing that could have happened to us, and an extraordinary opportunity. In short, this experience demonstrates, once again, that since there are so many events over which we have no control, we shouldn't overlook those that fall within the scope of our responsibilities. Let's learn to focus on what is within our power: doing absolutely everything possible to invent a better future for our communities.

BIBLIOGRAPHY

Books About Transition
Transition Network, The Essential Guide to Doing Transition: Getting Transition Started in Your Street, your Community, Town or Organization. 2017. (In several languages, free: http://transitionnetwork.org/resources/essential-guide-transition/)

About Permaculture and Food
Perrine and Charles Hervé-Gruyer, *Miraculous Abundance: One Quarter Acre, Two French Farmers and Enough Food to Feed the World* (with a foreword by Eliot Coleman), Chelsea Green Publishing, 2016.
David Holmgren, *Permaculture: Principles and Pathways Beyond Sustainability*, Permanent Publications, 2011.
Bill Mollison and David Holmgren, *Permaculture I.*, International Tree Crop Institute. USA, 1991.
Bill Mollison, *Permaculture II.*, Tagari, 1979.
Pamela Warhurst and Joanna Dobson, *Incredible! Plant Veg, Grow a Revolution*, Matador, 2014.

About Crisis and Solutions
Charles Dickens, *Great Expectations*, Penguin Classics, 2012.
Cyril Dion, *Tomorrow: All Over the Globe, Solutions Already Exist*, Actes Sud, 2017.
Julian Dobson, *How to Save our Town Centres. A Radical Agenda for the Future of High Streets*, Policy Press, 2015.
Richard Heinberg, *The End of Growth: Adapting to Our New Economic Reality*, New Society Publishers, 2011.
Richard L. Knight (ed.), *Aldo Leopold, and the Ecological Conscience*, Oxford University Press, 2011.
David Nobbs, *The Second Life of Sally Mottram*, Paperback, 2014.

Movies

Nils Aguilar, *Voices of Transition*, 2012 (http://voicesoftransition.org).

Transition Network, *In Transition 1.0*. Directed by Emma Goude, 2009 (available on Vimeo).

Transition Network, *In Transition 2.0*, Transition Network. Directed by Emma Goude, 2012 (www.intransitionmovie.com).

Gregory Greene, *The End of Suburbia: Oil Depletion and the Collapse of the American Dream*, The Electric Wallpaper Co., 2004 (http://www.endofsuburbia.com/).

Rebecca Hosking and Tim Green, *A Farm for the Future*, 2009 (also available on YouTube).

Faith Morgan, *The Power of Comunity: How Cuba Survived Peak Oil*, 2006 (available on YouTube).

Mélanie Laurent and Cyril Dion, *Tomorrow*, May 2017.

In the same series

Lionel Astruc, *Vandana Shiva: Creative Civil Disobedience*, 2017.
Cyril Dion, *Tomorrow*, 2017.
Emmanuel Druon, *Ecolonomy*, 2018.
Pierre Rabhi and Jacques Caplat, *Agroecology: An Ethical Life*, 2018.
Pierre Rabhi, *The Power of Restraint*, 2017.

Designed by
Atelier Graphique Actes Sud
and Printed in July 2017
by Normandie Roto Impression s.a.s.
61250 Lonrai
N° d'impression : 1701815
on paper made of wood from
sustainably managed forests
for Actes Sud
Le Méjan
Place Nina-Berberova
13200 Arles.

Legal deposit, first edition: October 2017
(Printed in France)